Grace Publishing
P.O. Box 1081
Freeland, WA
98249
1-800-282-5292

ISBN 1-893037-02-9 Well Being in Body, Mind and Spirit

IMPORTANT: This book is not intended to substitute
for the advice of physicians or other health care providers.
It offers information to help the reader cooperate with
health professionals in a joint approach to achievement of
optimal health.

Grace Publishing
$16.95

Praise for Jaya Sarada

Jaya is a masterful midwife for those of us searching for more. Her insights, clarity, and manner of BEING with you are all amazing gifts she gives freely.
Andreanna Vaughan, Nurse Practitioner

Jaya's wisdom, insight and depth of spiritual development is a gift to us all. She has the remarkable ability to translate the sublime into practical techniques that are easily accessible and invaluable in our daily lives.
Judyth Reichenberg-Ullman, ND. Co-author,
Mystics, Masters, Saints, and Sages: Stories of Enlightenment.

Jaya's loving devotion to the spiritual path shines through her personhood, her healing work and her writing. Jaya's adept use of kinesiology leads her directly to the areas of the body and its energy field that are in need of clearing or support. She is always right on target. Having been both a client and a student of Jaya's, she has augmented my own practice immensely as I've combined her meticulous and comprehensive methods with sound healing.
Dr. Lotus Linton Howard

It is from a place of peace from which Jaya Sarada brings forth her soul essence as a healer. Her gentle, loving care provides a sanctuary in which one can easily and trustingly open to receive that which is desired for healing. In over 10 years of knowing and working with Jaya, she has remained heart-full with pure intent in all she does.
Annapoorne, Counselor, Intuitive Reader, Integral Yoga Instructor

Also by Jaya Sarada:

Trust in Yourself – Messages from the Divine

The Path of Return – The Light of Parashakti

Life Essence Awakening – Energy Field Kinesiology for Transformation and Healing

Living Meditations

Contents

Chapter 8: Vibrational Medicine – continued

Acknowledgments

May this book offer you a path to Well Being in Body, Mind and Spirit and serve to awaken the living flame that resides in your heart. Attending to this sacred flame illuminates your journey home and nurtures the evolving love within your precious soul. May this love create peace and harmony and assist you to heal the root causes of suffering.

Deepest gratitude to my family and friends for the love and support you have given for the unfolding of my work.

To my dear friend Laurie Keith, who offered clarity and direction, and to Patricia my eternal sister for your friendship and hours of proofreading.

Special thank you to Judy and John Riclin for your help with the work, and furthermore, Judy for her beautiful illustrations.

Much love and gratitude to Karen Foster Wells for the gift of your amazing mandalas. They have found a home in my heart and work for over two decades.

Thank you, Ruth Pettis, for layout, proofreading, and indexing, and to Kathy Gambill for the cover design.

Benediction

Namaste, I salute the divinity within you

This work is dedicated to the living flame that resides in all hearts, guiding, protecting and nurturing the precious life force. Attending to this sacred flame illuminates our journey home, supporting the unfolding love and truth of our precious souls. May this love create peace and harmony and serve to end the cause of self-created suffering. May this book offer a path of Well Being for all and lead us to our greatest potential in body, mind and spirit.

Take a moment to relax, breathe, stretch. Prepare yourself for an inward journey of the soul. Breathe deeply. On each exhalation, let go of tensions, concerns, fatigue, thoughts.

Breathing in, allow the breath to fill any area that needs healing. Continue the slow, deep breathing. Your journey begins as a being of pure light, unconditioned by thought and emotion. The physical body is created as a vehicle of return. A divine child, you are Shakti, the evolving spirit surging through manifestation to find a way home to unconditional love, happiness, joy and peace. You discover a sense of self and personal power through the attainment of desires, cravings and attractions. The manifestation of your desires creates a search for something more, and the search for love continues. Deep inside your heart you hear a small voice saying, "Stop, stop seeking anything outside of yourself." You turn within and taste your eternal nature, the source of joy and peace. The path leads to the end of suffering, where you find a deepening presence awakening in your heart.

You hear the voice of the beloved within your heart and let go of burdens, preparing to enter the temple of light. You realize you are the witness of your life and see the miracle of perfection unfolding. Breathing in, you feel the grace that comes from entering life fully. Breathing out, empty and surrender, welcoming the beloved within. You affirm: I am not the body, or senses, nor mind. I am a divine being of pure energy. I Am that I am.

The journey leads you to deeper and deeper surrender, letting go of all obstacles that veil your true nature. The light of your soul awakens and becomes aware of a conscious presence that has been silently watching you throughout your life. This presence of being guides your soul to rest deeply in peace, the silence of the heart. Breathing in the love and wisdom of your heart, you rest in the presence of the beloved, sending this love into the world of all suffering beings. The love of the heart is the garden of your soul, where you and the beloved are one. In this oneness you take the path of Ahmisa, the gentleness of a deer, harmlessness.

With guidance, you open the Lotus of your soul, and awaken inner knowing, the point between opposites, beyond duality, into silence, wisdom and penetrating awareness. Shakti has traveled the path of evolving love to unite with Shiva, the Master of life. Through opening and transforming all limitations you celebrate the marriage of matter and spirit. This divine union, manifested, is no longer subject to the duality of life and is adorned with a thousand-petaled crown of jewels that opens to heaven. Shiva and Shakti, merged as one in the crown chakra, return to the sacred temple of the heart to rest eternally.

Preface

Though the term *paradigm shift* may be overused or cliche, that is exactly what is taking place powerfully now in health care. Scientists have confirmed that we really are made up of vibrating interconnected energy fields. When one accepts this model of what we are, many previously misunderstood phenomena begin to make perfect sense.

Disease occurs when there is a disturbance in the energy movement in the field or system. All treatments are effective to the degree that they can stimulate movement and balancing of the energy fields.

Alternative and complementary therapies have been so successful that today people make more visits to these types of providers than they do to their primary care physicians. Most of these are based on facilitating movement of the energy field on some level. Even many conventional medical treatments can be understood in terms of energy and fields as well as through biochemistry and mechanics.

The ramifications of acceptance of this paradigm reach out to every level of existence. No longer are we talking just about the body or just about health care. Because all fields are interconnected to some extent, we can no longer completely separate fields of knowledge. Heath care is intimately related to physics, psychology, spirituality, astronomy, consciousness, biochemistry and even history. We are vibrational beings carrying patterns of energy. Call them memory, neurological pain loops, belief systems, etc. that have been formed either through our experiences in life, through our environmental exposures, through our relationships with others and ourselves, through our families and even through the beliefs and experiences of our ancestors. These patterns both define who we are and limit who we are.

Jaya Sarada has created an amazingly efficient and direct road map, a powerful tool to uncover where some of our patterning doesn't serve our greater health, passion and purpose. With this tool we can not only consciously release some of the conditioning that inhibits our full expression and vitality; but we can open the door to awareness of who we really are and how truly powerful and beautiful we are as we experience the gifts of divine grace, spiritual attunement or whatever one's sacred path calls *connection to God*.

Laurie Keith, B.A., L.M.P.
Langley, Washington

Introduction

Well Being in Body, Mind and Spirit

In the Light of calm and steady self-awareness inner energies
wake up and work miracles without any effort on your part.

Sri Nisargadatte Maharshi

Well Being in Body, Mind and Spirit is an invitation to release anything in your life that is blocking your precious life force. It is a natural path to your divine spirit. To be well and vibrant on all levels, you must learn to look deep into the root cause of suffering. *Well Being in Body, Mind and Spirit* is loving all aspects of your being; the physical, emotional, mental and spiritual energy fields, and becoming a great caretaker of your soul.

Well Being is Vibrant Energy Field Health

Etheric Field Well Being: Strong, Light, Luminous, Active, Creative, Restful, Vital Field, Strong Immune Force, and Abundant Life Energy

Emotional Field Well Being: Joyous, Calm, Uplifting, Lightness, Happy, Vibrant, Positive, Unselfish Desires, Contentment

Mental Field Well Being: Positive Thoughts, Stable, Peaceful, Aware, Acceptance, Living in the Now, Power of Attention, Good-Self Esteem

Spiritual Well Being: Connected to Source, Attunement, Whole, Complete, Inner Freedom, Aware, Intuitive

When our energy fields are radiant and our life essence is intact, our authentic sense of self is strong. Intentional evolution occurs when we live life, aspiring for *Well Being in Body, Mind and Spirit.* Each energy field holds the potential for well being and collectively they build the foundation for the growth of our spiritual nature.

The first three energy fields, the etheric, emotional and mental planes form our personality selves. Our challenge in life is to realize we are not just our body, nor our emotions, nor our mind. The true essence of our being is realized in the spiritual energy fields. This understanding requires us to take the path of mastery, becoming attuned and aligned with the light of our soul.

Throughout our lives we are challenged to master our human weaknesses, to develop inner strength, courage and perseverance. There is a profound yearning to know more about ourselves, to deepen our understanding of our purpose as human beings. Through investigation into the nature of our true self, we can observe that the personality aspects of our being (what we know through time and memory) can no longer define who we are.

We initiate the mastery process by turning within, and listening to our soul following its guidance.

Our spiritual energy field holds the source of joy, spiritual will and freedom: the gifts of our life, our soul's birthright. The path of well being takes us into our sacred heart, a place of deep peace and silence where our vital force flows, nourishing our body, mind and emotions.

Our lifetime offers a wonderful opportunity to learn to love and care about ourselves as an integrated system of body, mind and soul. This requires purification of the personality nature of our being, where our emotional body is stilled and our mental body is in balance and inspired from our spiritual nature.

Our vital energy is essential for our well being. When it is flowing freely we experience an optimal level of health and wholeness. During times of stress, our vital force is affected and therefore we experience a depletion of energy on some level. Depending on the origin of the stress, it may affect us physically, emotionally, mentally or spiritually. When stress is unresolved we identify with thoughts, emotions and patterns that stem from the past. Given the art of seeing, we can use our awareness as a tool to look and see the root causes of our suffering, whether it be organic, emotional, mental or spiritual. Through our gifts of awareness we apply the healing power of love, to correct problems from the root cause.

During our lifetime, we can either let life's experiences defeat us or honor them as sacred pointers to our true reality. We observe how life is a movement of grace that is guiding us to optimal well being in body, mind and spirit. In this honoring we strengthen, expand and grow as we meet the challenges and tests that life presents. We become a co-creator with life and see that in all things are hidden blessings, pointing in the direction of self-understanding and self-realization. We are shown, through our daily life, where we need to apply the sacred and healing force of love, surrendering our personal will to this most humbling force, yielding to its direction and lessons in self-mastery.

Well Being in Body, Mind and Spirit is an invitation to become a spiritual warrior, skilled in energetically warding off discordant forces and challenges that life brings. We learn to guard and cherish our sacred energy as a most precious jewel. This jewel of consciousness within is our dearest companion as it guides us to a life of peace, wellness, divinity and great beauty. The essence of life is pure grace that leads us to understand the gifts of outer challenges and tests. When the gifts or lessons can be extracted from life's experiences, then our vital energy flows through our being and is not retained in memories that are unresolved.

Seeing the grace of life and learning the lessons of the soul allow us to live in the moment. In this freedom, we have the vitality to face the challenges of life without the encumbrance of the past. Lessons are learned by surrendering to our divine nature and realizing the purpose of this life is to evolve in the love and truth of our pure consciousness.

Our divine self is the background of our life. It witnesses our temporary nature riding the waves of pleasure and pain and all aspects of duality. The background remains silent, watchful and ever present as the temporary nature of life weaves a story of endless change. In healing the body, mind and emotions, we turn away from changing appearances and meet the eternal nature of our sacred heart. This meeting redirects us to love, peace, compassion and communion with our divine creator.

The healing force within each of us can uncover that which is vital, perfect and full of goodness. For this to occur we must learn to surrender and let go of the past and the identification with pain and pleasure. We must truthfully see the areas of our life that have been created from the web of mistaken identification. We must look at the way these webs have brought suffering to our life and contributed to the suffering of mankind. From this seeing, the deep compassion and the love of our heart awaken, releasing all things that are not of the highest good.

Well Being in Body, Mind and Spirit invites you on a journey through your luminous aura. Through the understanding that you are a multidimensional energy being, you can observe how your body, mind and emotions play an integral part of your well being.

Well Being in Body, Mind and Spirit offers you an in-depth study of the seven chakras as keys to your well being. This dynamic book looks at the energy anatomy and shares with you the amazing *Art of Kinesiology*, the science of muscle testing to answer questions regarding the condition being of your multidimensional energy fields. You will learn amazing methods in which to obtain *Yes or No* answers for your life questions.

Well Being in Body, Mind and Spirit has a complete Vibrational Medicine Toolbox: Bach Flowers, Essential Oils, Chakra Fragrances, Flower Essences, Color Healing, Crystal and Gemstones. It offers you instructions on how to use kinesiology or a pendulum to determine which Vibrational remedy will support your healing path.

Well Being in Body, Mind and Spirit offers you a complete manual on Energy Wellness Self Care: Breathing Visualizations, Daily Chakra Meditations, Energy Field Protection, Energy Exercises, Energy Tune-Up, Emotional Freedom Technique (Tapping for Energy Health) Healing Mudras, Healing Sounds and Mantras, AuraTouch and Chakra Balancing.

Well Being in Body, Mind and Spirit offers you Energy Testing Charts for Self Care Empowerment: Vitamins, Nutrition, Allergy, Minerals, Foods, Amino Acids, Trace Minerals, Tissue Salts, Endocrine Glands, Digestive Enzymes, Metals and Lifestyle.

Well Being in Body, Mind and Spirit also serves as introductory material to the new book *Life Essence Awakening – Energy Field Kinesiology for Transformation and Healing*, available through your local bookstores or Grace Publishing: 1-800-282-5292.

Chapter One:

Your Luminous Essence

Love says: "I am everything."
Wisdom says: "I am nothing."
Between the two my life flows.

      Nisargadatta Maharaj, **I Am That**

*O*ur *life essence* is composed of energy fields that surround the physical body and extend outward portraying our luminous aura. This subtle, unseen, energy that surrounds our being is an integral part of our existence. Each of the seven fields that make up our multidimensional energy system is a vehicle for our evolution to ever-greater creative expression as souls.

According to current scientific thought, there is a holographic energy template associated with the physical field. This holographic energy is characterized by a spectrum of energy bands radiating out from the physical. The first band of energy, the etheric field, is the cellular information that guides the cellular growth of the physical structure of the body. The next plane, the emotional, is a higher frequency and is involved in the expression and repression of emotion. The third plane is the mental field, the field of concrete thoughts, mind mixed with emotions, conditioning and beliefs. The remaining four fields have to do with intuition and spirit and are composed of higher frequencies that provide healing and transformation on a soul level.

The Aura and the Energy Fields

The word aura comes from the Greek word, *avra*, meaning breeze. The aura is the sum total of the seven fields of our human and divine nature. The spheres of energy surrounding the physical body progressively spiral outward forming our luminous energy fields. There are seven fields in the solar system, which relate to the seven fields of the human being. Our journey begins in a physical body – the vehicle to fully realize that within us lives a divine and eternal soul. Our inner being uses this vehicle to explore not only what it is to be human, but also what it is to be divine. Our physical and personality expressions come from the first four fields of consciousness: the physical, etheric, astral and mental. As we evolve past the limitations of our personal identity, we open the door to our true nature.

The Etheric Field

Science has shown that everything in nature has an atmosphere or electromagnetic field surrounding it. This energy duplicates all living organisms and is called the etheric field: a fluid-like substance visible as a band of light around the physical, protecting and shielding it from outside negative influences. The etheric underlies and interpenetrates every atom, cell and molecule of the physical field. The etheric field is the framework on which the physical body is built and is the source of vital force. The etheric energies move in fine channels closely related to the nervous system, nourishing the entire field with prana, the life force.

The etheric field is also called the health aura because it emanates strong or weak streams of vital force according to the well being of the individual. The electric energy of the health aura is seen as a luminous gray or violet mist that duplicates the physical field about a quarter of an inch from the skin. Another word for the health aura is ectoplasm, which is a term used to describe the etheric energy that constitutes the state between energy and matter. It determines our health as well as provides a protective force field that shields the field from negative influences. When the energy is strong the etheric field is smooth with streams of light emanating vertically from the physical field. When there is an imbalance in the system the rays will show signs of weakening and droop, reducing our ability to fight illness. The physical will then show signs of stress.

Unused etheric field energy is discharged from the pores and creates the luminous force field or health aura. Many alternative practitioners can detect imbalances through the condition of the health aura before they affect the physical. When imbalances are detected, holistic and preventative methods are applied to sustain, support and offer healing to strengthen the physical system.

The etheric field nurtures our blood, is the river of life, and is a transmitter of a vast aggregate of energies and forces. This vital force is responsible for the right functioning of our five senses and is a potent receiver of impressions, bringing the life force to all systems of the physical body.

The etheric field is an electromagnetic grid that weaves around the physical field. There are thousands of tiny nerves or nadis that cross each other throughout the field. These nadis are threads of life force that underlie every part of the body. Where they cross, especially along the spine, they form the chakras, which are energy gateways that can be described as wheels of light. The chakras are vital supports for the health of our multidimensional energy fields, affecting the way we feel physically, emotionally, mentally and spiritually.

The Emotional Field

Next, the emotional or astral field interpenetrates the etheric and is often seen as an aura of changing colors. As emotions, feelings and passions flow and change, so do the colors and shapes of the astral field. The emotional field can be viewed as the *Sea of Emotions* with water representing the uncontrollable nature of emotions. The biblical story of Jesus walking on the water (emotions) while rebuking the storm (mind) is an example of the kind of mastery he had over the aspects of emotions and mind that make up the lower self, the personality aspect of a human being. When we mistakenly identify the personality as our true self, we create a deep sense of separation from our source.

Between the etheric and the emotional field lies a protective sheath that prevents emotional energy from overwhelming the etheric. Injury to this sheath can be very dangerous and usually comes from emotional shock. Unharmonious forces, which penetrate the etheric through violence, anger or fear, tear the sheath and open one to illness. Drugs and alcohol can also tear the sheath and send poisons to the astral field. Since the etheric field is closely related to the emotional field, it is permeated at all times with emotions, which directly affect the physical state. When stress and emotional trauma occur in our life, damage first appears in the etheric field, weakening the physical field and making it vulnerable to illness. The mental field, the next energy plane, has a strong impact on the emotional field. Negative thought patterns create corresponding patterns of negative emotional stress; positive thought patterns create positive feelings. Of course, positive energy greatly improves the state of energy health. It is important to identify negative mental and emotional habits, resolve and release them.

After observing that we are truly multidimensional energy beings we can create health and wholeness through learning to detect imbalances in our energy fields and apply the corrections needed.

When the emotional field is in harmony with the soul and moral and mental development is of a high order, the aura, a visual expression of the emotional field, becomes bright and luminous and extends out to eighteen inches or more. When the emotional field expresses passions, emotions and desires that are out of harmony with the light of the soul, the aura becomes dark and murky, contracting to ten to twelve inches around the physical. Highly developed beings display large auras, showing the high degree of spiritual development that makes them candidates for initiation. Initiations in various spiritual traditions are gateways to the next level of spiritual development.

The emotional matter is a higher frequency of energy then etheric matter. It surrounds the etheric field and shows areas of congestion that come from negative thinking and ill emotions. It also reveals the condition of the etheric field. The emotional field acts as a bridge between the mental field and the etheric field. The emotional field makes sensation possible and acts as an independent vehicle of consciousness. Because the emotional field is connected to the mental field, our thoughts greatly influence our emotions as well as our physical well being.

The Mental Field

The mental field exists slightly beyond the emotional body. Mental energy comes through the crown center to let vibrations (impressions on the physical) of a higher nature pour through. The mental field provides a shield to protect the energy fields from imbalances and disease. This is the energy field where our affirmations, the spoken word, our choices, healing thoughts, and clear decisions play an important part in our healing and wellness process. When there are patterns of imbalance in the mental field stemming from negative thinking we are more susceptible to illness. When we strive for clear thoughts we transmit healing energy to the physical field via the spleen.

The energy of the mental field is constantly changing, moving rhythmically in response to thought. Good thoughts create an upward vibration and bad thoughts create a downward motion of the mental field. The mental field, when inspired from our higher or soul nature, expresses great beauty with moving iridescent light and color. Through the evolution of the intellect, the mental field becomes increasingly more radiant.

The mental field has two aspects, the higher mental and lower mental. This division is discussed in Sanskrit teachings, naming the lower mental Rupa, meaning having form. The lower mental field expresses through the personality in the form of concrete thoughts.

The higher aspect of the mental field, in Sanskrit, is called Arupa, meaning formlessness. This aspect of the mental field relates to intuition, perception and inspiration from our divine source. The higher mental is connected to the formless, eternal presence that resides within our soul and is not bound to a physical field for existence. We are simply sparks of this infinite life force and the higher mental is the field that carries us beyond time, thought, memory and form into our divine reality.

The lower mental expresses thoughts and emotions based on concrete knowledge of the personal self in relationship to the past. The lower mental is a vessel for the storage of memory, recording the sensations of pleasure or pain. The lower mind seeks to repeat the pleasurable or repel what is not pleasurable. Identification with our personality self is the aspect of our nature that is the greatest obstacle in our evolutionary path. Thoughts and emotions geared to self-importance and self-preservation obstruct the flow of our spiritual wisdom. The personality, or lower self, is attracted by the material world, perceiving it as true reality, perpetuating the wheel of cause and effect.

Truth, when perceived from our divine source is filtered from the spiritual to the mental fields and then our mind becomes an instrument of our soul. Our thoughts, actions and perceptions from the higher mental field access the love and wisdom of the heart and the knowledge of the higher world.

Deepening awareness shows us how emotions and thoughts play an integral part in understanding the key to good health and well being. Reflecting on the causes of illness and suffering we must take into account the totality of our being and how all parts are interconnected. There are many ways to purify and enhance our body, emotions, mind and spirit. When these fields communicate, integrate and create an upward mobility of consciousness, we experience a great vitality.

Web of Mind and Emotions
(The Kama-Manasic Web)

Within the emotional and lower mental fields we become bound to earth by our desires. This Kama-Manasic state (mix of mind and emotion) sets conditions for future incarnation. Many stay in this realm, not evolving past self-gratification into the light of the soul. The Kama-Manasic web, strengthened by the interplay of mind and emotions, creates veils that cloud our true nature.

Happiness is our deepest quest, but we seek this happiness out of the temporary aspects of life, not realizing the impermanence of the search. The energy fields that surround us offer keys to the discovery of our true *life essence*. We search for temporary fulfillment of our bodies, which can never quench the thirst of our endless desires. We search for emotional fulfillment, not realizing that our emotions are constantly changing from pleasure to pain and then from pain to pleasure. Then there is a search for the true self in the realm of thought

and mind, but again we find that everything changes in our mind. Our search for the long-lost sense of self takes us into the etheric field where we experience our vital force; to our emotional field where we experience our passions, power, and desires; to the mental field where we experience the power of our mind and thoughts. Our desires are rooted in our emotional field and we often set out to obtain gratification at any cost. We are convinced that our desire and thought processes are the truth of truths and often will stop at nothing to obtain a particular desire. The desires obtained are temporary and the search for pleasure that often results in pain continues until we turn within to the real source of happiness. When the desire is fueled with thoughts from the mental field, an energetic web is created that becomes quite difficult to overcome. This is the Kama-Manasic web, the root of karma and reincarnation.

For most, the center of consciousness is located in the emotional field where the ordinary person is enslaved by thought tainted with emotions. Average humanity is submerged in the illusions of the emotional field. The emotions of anger, worry, fear, etc. create a continuous irritation of the etheric field, which affects the physical.

The Energy Fields and Their Functions

Physical: energy field that relates to the element earth and corresponds to the root chakra, the endocrine glands and functions energetically to provide a ground for being.

Etheric: relates to the element water and corresponds to the navel chakra, the testes in males and the ovaries in females and is the field of physical creativity.

Emotional: relates to the element fire and corresponds to the solar plexus chakra; externalizes as the pancreas and expresses personal power.

Mental: associated with the element air and corresponds to the heart chakra; externalizes as the thymus gland; expresses divine power and guides us to surrender our personal will.

Causal: relates to the element of ether and corresponds to the throat chakra; externalizes as the thyroid gland and is the field of spiritual expression.

Monadic: relates to the sixth sense and corresponds to the third eye chakra. The monadic field develops a sense of knowing, intuition and union of duality and externalizes as the pituitary gland.

Adi: pure consciousness, this field corresponds to the crown chakra. The Adi field functions to return our consciousness to oneness and integration. Externalizes as the pineal gland.

The Causal Field –The Temple of Our Soul

The causal, celestial or intuitional field extends beyond the mental field about eighteen inches, in an ovoid shape that surrounds the physical field. The energy of this field is radiant and full of color according to our development. The more evolved we become, the more luminous the colors of this energy field. The causal field holds the essence of our higher intuition and is also known as the celestial field because it is composed of the vibrations of our soul's light and wisdom. This field is our Sacred Auric Egg, or the seed body, holding the blueprint of all future incarnations.

The causal field functions as a vehicle for the true self to express the divine law of love, wisdom and truth. The Akashic records, the records of nature and stories of our soul, are held within the causal field. These stories are strung like pearls along the sacred thread, or Sutratma, and bring forth the strengths and attributes the soul has acquired through all of life's experiences.

The causal field holds this thread, the records of our lifetimes, and determines the condition of future incarnations. This thread of our being weaves our stories and holds the essence of our evolving love, truth and goodness that is brought from each lifetime into our soul until we perfect ourselves as human beings. The true self uses the pearls of existence and seeks rebirth to further the evolution of God consciousness; each lifetime forming a new vehicle to refine or develop certain soul qualities and strengths. This intention, called Trishna in Sanskrit, is a thirst that attracts us to life experiences that provide soul strength on our homeward journey. Our soul's development is orchestrated by the great mystery of life, a continuous evolution into the consciousness of love and light.

Throughout all births the essence of our being remains whole, and in truth, one with the source of pure consciousness. The *Antahkarana*, meaning bridge of light, connects our personality with our soul. Our inner development by way of this bridge channels the part of us that has been awakened into the part that needs to be awakened. The Antahkarana is constructed through the realization of our true nature. When we no longer identify with our temporary human nature of thoughts, emotions and sensations, as a separate sense of self, the bridge dissolves and we become one consciousness. The intuitive field not only holds the answers to our life's lessons and questions, it also opens the door to our inner guide or master teacher. This loving guide becomes ours when we turn our attention from the belief in our separate self, to the eternal essence of our heart. Our inner guide offers assistance in the understanding and mastery of our personality nature.

There are four sheaths that clothe the soul and create the energy being that we are. The sheaths are veils that cover and connect the energy fields. The first sheath is the physical field and is called the food sheath. It is fed only by food. The second sheath is related to the etheric and is called the vitality sheath. It is fueled by prana. The third is related to our mind and emotions (the lower mental and emotional field together) and is called the feeling sheath. It is fed only by feelings. The fourth field is the causal, called the discriminating sheath because it has the function of pure intelligence based on intuition and soul wisdom. This level of intelligence is not affected by the senses, but operates according to divine will and creative power. The source of this intelligence is not the world or the senses, nor is it based on the knowledge of the personality but the pure wisdom of the divine source.

The causal field is the creative power of the soul, which allows all things to spring forth by one-pointed thought, the source of all magic. When an idea comes from the level of the soul and is deeply concentrated upon, it is manifested. The higher mind expresses positive, creative thought that comes from the source of our consciousness.

The causal, also called intuitive field is the temple of our true essence, where spirit and matter are unified, and is beyond the limitations of human consciousness. The pure consciousness of the soul is devoted to divine essence, whereas the lower mind is focused on details of the physical field. Thoughts generated from the higher mind are expressed in principles that have a powerful effect on life. These principles, perceived by the soul, reflect the divine wisdom found in the spiritual heart.

The records of all incarnations are stored in the causal body. These seeds which are our **Karma** lie dormant until we are reborn again. In each new physical manifestation these seeds have to be sown to bring to fruition the completion of past actions. These seeds, in Sanskrit called Skandas, are deep scars upon the soul that determine the conditions of the next incarnation. Skandas represent desires, impulses and obligations that cause a being to forever stay on the wheel of cause and effect.

The causal or celestial field is the temple of the divine spark and is called the Monad. Love is the force and the source of this spark. The Monad, the spark of divinity that awakens our heart, leads us beyond the limitations of birth to eternity. Our true essence is this divine spark – eternal, whole and untouched by disease and disharmony.

Chapter Two:

Life Essence
Pathways

*You will never be satisfied until you find out
that you are what you are seeking.*

Nisargadatta Maharaj, I Am That

*T*hrough the etheric field we are an integral part of the entire kingdom of nature. A force of energy surrounds every living thing. Rays emanate from the aura's core just as solar rays emanate from the sun. The thousands of pathways of life forces, the nadis, keep energy flowing to the physical from the universal life force and the outer world: the sun, the energy fields and the seven cosmic rays. The soul uses these channels to pour life energy into the system.

Interlaced through the etheric field an energy stream, called the silver cord, links the physical and astral fields. An intricate weaving of subtle energies within the etheric, the silver cord connects all the vital centers, keeping us grounded through the many lessons and experiences of life.

The silver cord, or Sutratma, incarnates at the beginning of a lifetime and infuses the physical with the life force through the blood stream. This sacred cord unifies the energy bodies and is anchored in the heart center. The silver cord makes contact with the soul through evolution to the mental field. The pearls of human existence, containing the seeds for future births, are strung along this cord. The Sutratma is the central channel where the flow of life force travels on the energetic path of return connecting our personal self to our divine spirit.

A threefold thread runs along the spinal column: the Ida, Pingala and Sushumna, forming the path of life. The Sushumna is called the creative thread, a cord that links the center at the base of the spine and is anchored in the throat center. The Ida follows the left side of the spine and is the lunar channel, related to the love and wisdom aspect of our being. The Pingala is located on the right of the spine and is the solar nadi, related to matter and intelligence. The Sushumna is located within the spinal column and is related to the father or "will aspect" of love. The Sushumna is the most important nadi, the channel through which our soul energy travels. The creative thread is responsible for the develop-ment of the personality. As it gradually widens through evolution and, through conscious awakening, the bridge of light, or *Antahkarana*, forms. This conscious awakening is the outcome of fusion between our personality and soul, opening a pathway to divine consciousness.

The pathways of the Ida, Pingala and Sushumna relate to three centers: the solar plexus, which is related to the impulse of desire in life, creative urges and the physical sun; the heart center, which is related to the impulse of love and divine expression; and the head center, which is related to the will to live.

The *Antahkarana*, the consciousness thread, is the inner organ that connects the personality with the soul. Antahkarana means bridge. Anchored in the heart center and reaching to the crown center, this bridge of light is built as one

awakens and evolves, until the entire being is linked in an integrated expression of divine consciousness. This process, called continuity of consciousness, is where the human soul awakens as an entity on the physical field, using the etheric, emotional and mental fields as vehicles of soul expression.

The life force begins in the etheric field, which represents a sense of being-ness, an acceptance of life and trust in its process. Holding this awareness in daily consciousness brings the etheric field into a healthy balance. The next field of consciousness, the emotional, is the plane of desires, emotions, feelings and sentience. Through life's journey we must learn to integrate the emotional field with the etheric field to create an unblocked flow of feelings throughout our heart and soul.

The mental field is the bridge between the emotions and the higher planes of spiritual consciousness. The mind, when silent and receptive, takes in impressions and guidance from the soul and passes them on to the emotional and etheric fields and all are infused with the energy of light, love and wisdom.

Kundalini Energy

A unique energy system that activates the energies of the chakras and assists us in awakening to our higher consciousness is called Kundalini. This powerful yet often dormant energy is stored in the root, or base chakra. The Kundalini energy can activate and align all the major chakras with the higher centers, bringing illumination and spiritual enlightenment to our beings. Through the proper sequence of chakra transformation and release of energy over time, the Kundalini begins to awaken. When traumatic emotional events occur which hold back our growth there is a corresponding block in one of the chakras. Energy blocks impede the natural flow of the creative Kundalini energies that rise up the spinal cord to the higher chakras. Daily meditation raises the Kundalini, and imparts the emotional and spiritual lessons related to particular chakras.

We begin the path of awakening by learning to be a witness, turning within to listen to the voice of the heart along with the wisdom of our inner being and releasing the faulty perception of the self. The Kundalini energy is the aspect of us that awakens as we become self-realized. This sacred energy can be viewed as the fire of our being. Everything in its path is purified.

Shiva and Shakti Unity of Duality

Kundalini is the rising or awakening of our inner Shakti (energy) from its latent state. The root word, Kundal means to coil, depicting a snakelike energy, which lies dormant at the base of the spine in the root chakra. Kundalini Shakti is the feminine energy of our innate power. A powerful electric current, Kundalini Shakti moves through the chakras along the spine. It is awakened through change in consciousness as well as through spiritual exercises, dance, yoga and music. Kundalini, although dormant in most people, has a surging force that propels us to awaken our being to merge with our source of pure consciousness.

Our divine aspect, or Shiva energy, resides in the crown chakra and holds our spiritual nature. Shakti, residing in the root chakra, is the aspect of our being that relates to form and is our evolving nature. Shakti travels upward to merge with Shiva in a marriage of spirit and matter. Through this union we touch unconditional love and joy. Our journey as souls leads us through the energy fields, opening the chakras and lifting the veil to our pure consciousness. The chakras open along the spine, one by one, through the transformation of our inner being. Our journey leads past the survival aspects of the first three centers of the personality into the doorway of the heart. The journey becomes lighter as the ascension process takes us into the throat chakra, where the rhythms of our true nature are expressed through sound.

When the energy opens along the passageway of the Sushumna, it pulls and pushes, disentangling the knots of each chakra and bringing profound transformation. The journey continues to the third eye wisdom center where we awaken to our true nature. At this point, all duality ceases and we may experience a cosmic unity as the Kundalini Shakti, the matter aspect of energy, merges with Shiva, the energy of spirit. This awakening of true love, wisdom and will is fully realized in the crown chakra and rests in the temple of the heart. With all chakras open and fully energized the journey is complete and all experiences are integrated transcending time, space and form.

Until one is committed there is hesi-
tancy, the chance to draw back, always
ineffectiveness. Concerning all acts of
initiative (and creation), there is one
elementary truth, the ignorance of
which kills countless ideas and splen-
did plans; that the moment one defi-
nitely commits oneself, then Provi-
dence moves too. All sorts of things
occur to help one that would never
otherwise have occurred. A whole
stream of events issues from the
decision, raising in one's favor all
manner of unforeseen incidents and
meetings and material assistance,
which no man could have dreamt would
have come his way.

William Hutchison Murray

Chapter Three:

Our Breath –
One Precious Life

There is only life.
There is nobody who lives a life.

> *Nisargadatta Maharaj,* I Am That

*T*he breath is a powerful tool to realize our true nature and the divine in all of life. The word Pranayama is formed from three Sanskrit roots: pra – meaning first, na – meaning energy, ayama – meaning expansion. Seeing the illusory, temporary nature of life, we can just smile and breathe out. Through the realization of our eternal being we breathe in, affirming that awareness in all the moments of life. A slow steady breath of receiving and of letting go will guide us toward a life of peace and beauty.

Breathing in the essence of life, we learn about ourselves and listen to our body rhythm. Breathing opens our reflective consciousness and helps us to see past impressions that trap us. Exhalation can be used to let go of past psychological holding, renewing our vital force.

Improper breathing weakens the function of almost every organ in the physical body. When our breathing is shallow we become more susceptible to the full spectrum of illness – headaches, depression and constipation, emotional and mental disorders. Many researchers believe that bad breathing habits also contribute to life-threatening diseases such as cancer and heart disease. Poor breathing reduces the efficiency of the lungs, impeding oxygen flow to the cells and diminishes energy needed for normal functioning, healing and growth.

The breath is vital in supporting us in our daily challenges. Deep breathing increases our vital force; all of our senses come alive and are transformed. Our breathing gives us a spaciousness to observe where we feel heavy and where we can apply our healing light to release ease unwanted burdens. Breathing takes us back to our source and opens us to a sense of harmony with the universal rhythm. Proper breathing clears our energy channels and opens our system to a healing light that affects all aspects of our body, mind and emotions.

The Breath and the Vital Centers

The Ida, the Pingala and the Sushumna, the three main channels of life energy, carry the vital force to all areas of our body, mind and emotions. These channels depend on the life force breath to heal and balance the system. The Ida and Pingala, corresponding to the autonomic nervous system, are responsible for the maintenance of the vital essence throughout the body. The Sushumna is related to the central nervous system and is the channel for the Kundalini Shakti. The Pingala flows along the right side of the Sushumna and is related to the sun. It has the yang qualities of aggression, logic, analytical thinking, outer direction, rationality, objectivity, heat, masculinity, mathematics and verbal activities. The Ida flows along the left side of the Sushumna and is related to the moon. It has yin qualities such as calmness, intuition, holism, inner direction, emotional subjectivity, femininity and coolness. The energy channels of the Ida and Pingala flow from the base chakra, weave up the spine in a snakelike manner and unite in the third eye center. The Sushumna is the pathway of the breath, our divine force that runs along the spine.

The vital centers are located along the Sushumna channel and are energized by the prana they receive. Beginning in the base chakra the breath flows upward to the solar plexus and unites with the higher prana flowing downward from the crown chakra. These two forces, the apana, meaning breath flowing upward and prana, meaning breath flowing downward, form a duality of psychic energy creating a knot in the solar plexus chakra. This knot forms when we contract our breathing, holding on to a false identification that is rooted in suffering. Through the process of releasing our old identifications, we begin to open the sacred heart center and this knot becomes free. Breathing has a very important relationship to the opening of the heart center that serves our purpose of letting go of the past. Through our breathing we can practice this art of letting go; as we exhale we let go of the past and as we inhale we welcome the unknown mystery of life.

The Breath and Energy Field Healing

Breathing habits reflect the areas of our personal holdings and where we contract and identify with passing appearances. When we exhale we can learn to let go of all concerns and return to our natural state of contentment and stillness. When we inhale we can observe where we contract, identifying with the passing nature of life, e.g. our thoughts and emotions, and then we can return to the art of letting go through exhalation.

Within each chakra lie keys to our unfolding and our breath carries these keys. The lower back, lower abdomen and pelvic areas carry information about our roots, our family, our origin, our survival needs and our sense of grounding. Breathing deeply into the root chakra helps to keep us feeling grounded and balanced. The navel chakra holds information about our sense of self, our relationships, physical energy and creativity. Breathing deeply, along with deep exhalations, assists our second chakra to stay balanced as well as opens us to our vital force energy. Our solar plexus chakra holds information about how we use our sense of power and helps us unite our mind with our heart.

Breathing deeply relaxes our struggle for personal power. Our throat chakra opens as we breathe in and exhale, we feel the current of energy from the lower chakras and direct this energy upward and out the crown center. When this current is flowing freely we can feel confident to speak and walk our truth.

Breathing deeply and exhaling fully allows our full energy to circulate up the chakras and through the crown. Then we feel we are in a circle of vibrant light. The third eye chakra softens and opens as the pranic energy moves up and bathes the inner eye in the warm wind of our breath. The third eye chakra tells the story of who we are and where we came from to help us meet our celestial nature. Holding the stories of all our births, the crown chakra creates a crown of glory as it opens and connects with the divine source when we breathe deep and exhale through the crown center.

Inharmonious emotions such as anger, fear, guilt, and grief are poisons that enter our system if not released by the breath. Shallow breathing harbors these negative emotions in our energy field until there is a deep exhalation and affirmation of letting go. By observing any negative emotions or limiting thought that has entered our energy field, we can learn to seek the root cause and then release the disturbance through the breath.

Positive emotions and thoughts such as joy, peace, and contentment sustain our health and well being. Negative emotions and thoughts create disturbances that affect our energy field eventually leading to disease. We can learn to exhale what is no longer serving us and inhale the qualities and principles of life we need. Breathing deeply creates strength in our energy field and shields us from negative thinking. Breathing with the energy of expanding opens us to our intuitive field and allows us to meet our true nature. The art of breathing holds the key to all processes in healing the body, mind and spirit.

Conscious breathing assists us on the path of mastery, teaching how to let go and receive our soul's wisdom. When our emotional or mental energy field is disturbed our breath can take us to a place of stillness where passing thoughts and emotions are dissolved.

When disturbed, our emotions or thoughts are like passing clouds in the sky. Breathing assists us in remaining centered and calm. Through the quiet mind we can choose peace rather than problems or conflict and release personal holdings. Our deep exhalation process provides the tools necessary to surrender the most difficult and challenging experiences.

Remaining conscious of our true nature, remembering who we are – these are essential in working with the energy fields. We then can use all of life's experience as a gift to remain in peace and harmony, our intention to live free from personal suffering.

Chapter Four:

Chakras – Turning the Keys to Awakening

*The state of witnessing is full of power,
there is nothing passive about it.*

Nisargadatta Maharaj, **I Am That**

Chakra is Sanskrit for wheel of light. Each chakra is a whirling center of vital energy shaped like a cone. The chakras are found along the spinal cord or Sushumna, the energetic channel that runs along the spine from the root chakra located at the base of the spine to the crown chakra which is at the crown of the head. The chakras energize, control and maintain proper function of our body, mind and emotions.

Nadis are nerve-like channels that carry our spiritual and vital energies to the energy fields. Where they intersect, they form a lotus with unfolding petals – a chakra. The number of petals varies according to the number of nadis. When the chakra and the petals are facing downward, the energy is undergoing a transformation process. The transformation occurs when we learn the lessons of a particular chakra and receive the energy to proceed in the ascension process. The petals turn up as we ascend to the next level of consciousness.

The chakras below the heart move in a counterclockwise manner in response to the downward pull of earth's gravity. The purpose of the lower chakras is to turn clockwise in harmony with the upper chakras. Upon awakening to our true self, the light of our consciousness pierces the center of the chakra involved and opens it to the divine essence. Each chakra contains a lesson and has a deep and profound purpose – to assist us on our spiritual path.

These gateways to our soul are our centers of light and protection and allow accumulated energy to exist or enter the system under the direction of soul power. The chakras play an important role in the etheric, emotional, mental and spiritual fields of consciousness. They are the doors to understanding ourselves on all levels.

Chakras are the regulators of the life force, providing major points of contact with the outside world and reception of impressions from the higher realms. There are seven major chakras in the etheric field. Each plays a part in nourishing and sustaining the nervous system, organs and endocrine glands. The etheric chakras are different from the emotional and mental chakras. They keep the vital energy of the physical body balanced and healthy. These chakras are essential to the life of the etheric and radiate according to the development and health of the individual. The etheric chakras influence the vitality of the whole system. They distribute prana throughout the etheric field, which then brings the life force to the physical. The chakras also function as communicators or trans-mitters from one energy field to the other – for example, the etheric field to the emotional field, emotional field to the mental field, and the mental field to the spiritual field.

There are four main chakras in the body and three in the head. The root chakra is the seat of the physical body, the navel center the seat of the etheric field, the solar plexus chakra the seat of the emotional field, the heart chakra the seat of the lower mental field, the throat chakra the seat of the higher mental field, the third eye chakra the seat of the intuitive field, and the crown center the seat of the spiritual field. The solar plexus, navel, and root are related to our personality nature and function in relationship to our physical survival, needs, and wants. They are also considered our power centers because they control the physical senses, express the tendencies of the personality and initiate the desires of clinging, craving, possessing, having and rejecting. The heart chakra is consid-ered the bridge of light between the physical (those below the heart) and the spiritual (those above the heart). The heart, throat, third eye and crown are the transcendental chakras of the soul and higher mind and are related to our higher self. Their function is to help us express, expand and deepen ourselves, allowing us to become integrated beings of light.

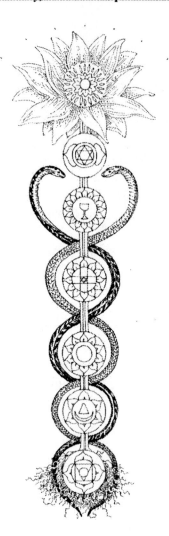

The first three chakras – root, navel and solar plexus – are the testing zones of our spiritual being. The solar plexus chakra provides the key to transforming our personal will into divine will, for it is within that center that the battle between the personality and the divine self takes place. When we let go of the struggle to maintain our separate individual self we open the door to the heart chakra where we meet our true nature. The root chakra is our foundation or ground for being. When balanced it reflects the needed stability, security and energy for our life's journey. We welcome the assignment given by the universe and trust that our life is a gift and an opportunity to evolve in love. Through our relationship with our God or crown chakra, we infuse our being with trust and security from a long-lasting source.

After creating a strong foundation in the root chakra, we journey into the consciousness of the navel chakra. This is the chakra of our physical vitality and expression in the physical world and our feeling self. It opens and is balanced naturally through the throat chakra. The experience of the solar plexus chakra brings us lessons in personal power, judgments, opinions and self-mastery. The heart chakra assists us along our journey to transform our personal power with the power of our divine source and teaches the art of surrender and the meaning of the affirmation, "Thy will be done."

Transcending the lower chakras opens the door to our spiritual nature. The throat center awakens as we begin to express our truth; divine miracles come from the spoken word. The heart chakra translates the message of compassion, surrender and letting go through evolving love. The wisdom of the third eye chakra shines with the light of cosmic consciousness.

When the chakras are blended and integrated they are instruments of divine power and glory. In a state of illumination the chakras are like jewels strung along the Sushumna, the life force that flows up the spine. Our chakras represent our state of consciousness and are indicators of the need to apply the healing attention of love. They are the tools for transformation, a map to our true self. We must carefully look at memories that we hold in the lower chakras. Once we release the past, the crown chakra can take its rightful place as the master of all the others, integrating and infusing us with divine light.

The Chakras and the Elements

The first three chakras make up the aspects of the personality. Related to earth, water and fire, they are associated with physical survival. The next three chakras relate to air, light and an integration of all elements, making up the spiritual aspect of our being.

The **root chakra:** Muladhara, meaning support at the root, is located at the base of the spine. With four petals of fiery red and orange tinged with gold and yellow, this chakra is a whirling vortex of energy flowing into the reproductive organs. Related to the earth element it energizes the sexual organs and external-izes as adrenal glands, governing the spine and kidneys. Kundalini, the serpent fire, resides here.

The **navel chakra:** Svadhisthana, meaning sweetness, is located at the midpoint of the sacrum. Related to the etheric field, this chakra externalizes as the repro-ductive glands and governs the reproductive system. The navel chakra is related to the water element and has six vermilion petals. The life force circulates from

CROWN

THIRD
EYE

THROAT

HEART

SOLAR
PLEXUS

NAVEL

ROOT

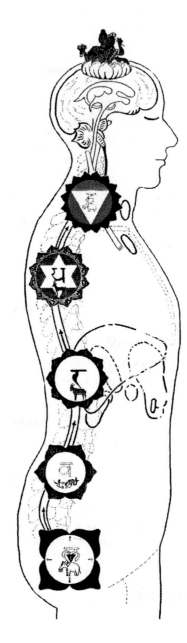

this chakra with the purpose of nurturing the physical creative force. Energies come into the field through the spleen and then are distributed to the remaining chakras.

The **solar plexus chakra:** Manipura, meaning lustrous gem, is related to the emotional field and affects the digestive system. This third chakra corresponds to the liver, kidneys and large intestine and is associated with feelings and emotions. Because Manipura is the power center of the physical field, where instincts and survival play an important role, it is easily exhausted. Predominantly yellow, this lotus has ten petals. The solar plexus chakra is related to the element fire.

The **heart chakra:** Anahata, meaning pure, untouched, is located behind the heart in the dorsal spine. Its twelve petals are a golden green color for healing or a rose pink for divine love. It externalizes as the thymus and governs the heart, circulation and blood. The energy of the heart corresponds to the compassion and love of the Buddha or Christ. The heart chakra is related to the life prana and the element of air.

The **throat chakra:** Visuddha, meaning purification, has sixteen petals of whirling blue and other colored energies. Located at the base of the neck, Visuddha governs the vocal chords, bronchia, lungs and digestive tract and externalizes as the thyroid and parathyroid glands. It is called the chakra of miracles for its connection with the powers of life and its ability to express intelligence through the spoken word. The throat chakra is related to the element of sound.

The **third eye chakra:** Ajna, meaning to know or perceive is located between the eyebrows on the forehead. It governs the eyes, teeth, sinuses, lower brain and the brain stem. The ajna chakra has two main petals of intense white with hues of purplish blue and violet and is related to the pineal gland and etheric sight. When aligned with the soul it brings clear thinking and vision, intuition and truth. This chakra is related to the element of light, where visualization becomes the gift through manifestation. Opening this chakra merges the dual nature so life is unified and whole.

The **crown chakra:** Sahashara, meaning thousand-petaled lotus, is located on the crown of the head. It governs the brain and nervous system and externalizes as the pineal gland. Through union and harmony of the heart and crown chakras love, will, and intelligence are balanced, opening the channel for the soul.

The Root Chakra –
Our Ground of Being

With a strong foundation we become willing participants in physical existence, cooperating with the forces of mother earth. The root chakra, Muladhara, meaning support at the root, provides us with keys to our life purpose. In the root center we hold the information about our family of origin and ancestral memories. Any damage can be healed through affirming our purpose and value as an evolving self. The lessons of the root center teach us to release old programs and conditioning that retain our energy in an untransformed state. Reaffirming our sense of trust and safety with life's processes and lessons builds an inner foundation of strength and an unconditional relationship to life.

The home of our basic instincts, the root chakra drives us to find sexual unity, passion and the fire of life. This fire gives stability, power and the instinct to survive and deepens our relationship with joy and gratitude for being alive.

A vortex of primal force, this chakra can create or destroy. When our energies are positive, optimistic, and life-affirming, the root center is balanced. When we feel disconnected, scattered and not present in life, we are not in balance. The root strives for harmony with the spiritual centers by reaching for the divine while stabilizing and grounding on the earth.

When this chakra is weak it manifests self-centeredness, anger and fear rooted in the survival instinct. Worry is an expression of an unbalanced root chakra; feeling insecure in the world where everyday life tends to feel burdensome. When balanced we feel confident and safe in our lives.

In order to maintain balance, the root chakra must be in harmony with the third eye and crown chakras. Working with the higher centers in our transformation process we create a new sense of grounding. Integration of our lower three chakras with the chakras of our soul reconnects us with our divine purpose in life. The crown center brings a security that is everlasting as it connects us with the divine creator of life. The third eye center brings our clear vision and connects us with the wisdom to tell the real from the unreal.

The Root Chakra Chart

Muladhara
Meaning the keeper of the beginning, the bearer of the foundation, the support at the root

Location: Base of spine between anus and genitals

Physical Correspondence: Bones, skeletal structure, spine

Physical Dysfunctions: Sciatica pain, lower back pain

Subtle Body: Physical/Etheric

Glandular Connection: Adrenals, controls all solid parts, spinal column, bones, teeth, nails, anus, rectum, colon, prostate, glands, blood, building of cells

Emotional Plane: Primary emotions: fear-released through a deep sense of security and trust. Other emotions: depression, confusion, feeling off-center, not belonging, obsessions released through a deep sense of stillness.

Mental Plane: A strong sense of self, secure with little or no self-doubt; stillness

Color: Fiery red

Petals: 4

Element: Earth

Symbol: Elephant of earthly abundance and good fortune, four red petals around a square containing a downward pointing triangle that represents the relationship to earth energies and karma

Animal Correspondence: Elephant

Sense: Smell

Fragrance: Cloves, cedar, patchouli, myrrh, musk

Ayurvedic oils: Ginger, vetiver

Healing Stones: Agate, hematite, blood jasper, garnet, ruby, tiger-eye blood-stone, smoky quartz, onyx

Sounds: Vowel C spoken in lower c

Mantra: LAM

Words to create healing affirmations: Responsibility, nurturance, abundance, trust, security, safety, stability, oneness, unity, connection with source, empowerment (letting go of being a victim), boundaries, limitations

Verb: To have

Yoga Postures: Bridge Pose, Half Locust, Full Locust, Head to Knee pose

Balanced Chakra: Deep trust in life, inner gratitude, life energy intact, connection with nature, trust in nature's laws, understanding life's changing ebb and flow.

Unbalanced Chakra: Self-centered, insecurity, possessiveness, lack of trust, feling ungrounded.

The Navel Chakra –
The Sea of Emotions

The navel chakra is called Svadhisthana in Sanskrit, meaning dwelling place of the self or sweetness. This chakra produces and assimilates internal energy received through air and food and distributes it from the spleen to the meridians and the vital force throughout all areas of the physical body.

Corresponding to water, the second chakra cleanses the body and mind of lower impulses and physical toxins. On the physical level the kidneys and bladder are strengthened and on an emotional level, emotions are centered and purified.

When in balance, the navel chakra creates a sense of abundance and appreciation for what life brings. This chakra is considered the seat of Shakti, where our physical, sexual and creative energy is expressed, the place of life, conception, change and movement. It can be visualized as a bright sphere of radiant orange light bringing forth creative energies and ideas. This chakra holds the magical wonder of our being and is related to the ages of eight to fourteen, when we most experience life's sweetness and unconditional joy.

The navel chakra represents change, duality, movement, flexibility and creative flow. When we energetically tune into this center we can observe that our lives are best served when we experience life in an unconditional manner. When balanced, this chakra represents a reservoir of fluid movement in all aspects of our life, flowing with life's changes.

The navel chakra is depicted as a six-petal lotus that relates to the six passions of lust, anger, greed, deceit, pride and envy. The navel chakra can be damaged and blocked by misuse and misunderstanding of sexual energy resulting in weakened physical stamina that attracts illness. Through mastery we can overcome these qualities and open to our full potential as human beings. The transformation of these emotions assists us in the evolution to our heart.

The energy of the navel chakra works closely with the ajna, or third eye chakra. Awakening our inner eye to develop discernment assists us in mastering the challenges of the navel. Our inner eye creates a direct stream of consciousness to integrate emotions, desires, pleasures and feelings with our higher knowing and our intention for wholeness.

The
Navel Chakra
Chart

Svadhisthana
Meaning sweetness, self-abode,
where the vital force resides.

Location: Lower lumbar area, lower abdomen, between navel and genitals

Physical Correspondence: Sex organs, bladder, kidney, circulation system, vital force, sacral plexus, sacral vertebra, liquids of the body

Physical Dysfunctions: Kidney, bladder problems, circulation and skin issues, lower back pain, sex organs, small intestine.

Subtle Body: Etheric

Glandular Connection: Ovaries, testicles, reproductive organs; controls pelvic area, sex organs, potency, fluid functions, kidneys and bladder.

Emotional Plane: Desire, passion; ability to be comfortable with feelings, good self-esteem, healthy sexual attitude, physical creativity, emotional instability

Mental Plane: Emotional principle (which work through the senses) understanding the duality of the world, working with opposites.

Color: Orange

Petals: 6

Element: Water

Symbol: White crescent moon, six orange petals containing a second lotus flower and a crescent moon

Animal Correspondence: Makara, a fish tailed alligator, fish and sea creatures

Sense: Hearing

Fragrance: Ylang ylang, sandalwood, jasmine and rose

Ayurvedic Oils: Cedar, sage, patchouli

Healing Stones: Carnelian, moonstone, citrine, topaz, coral, tourmaline

Sounds: Sound and Vowels O sung in D

Mantra: VAM

Words to create healing affirmations: Happiness, fulfilled, acceptance of self and others, worthy, creative, expressive, honor, nurture, listen to feelings, working in harmony with truth and inner vision, vital energy intact, moving freely with ease through the world, acceptance of change

Verbs: I feel, I open, I am

Yoga Postures: Pelvic Rock, Leg Lifts, Hip Circles

Balanced Chakra: Harmonious feelings, healthy sexual feelings, creative expression, considerate and friendly, happily connected to life, healthy, vibrant energy, secure in oneself, good self esteem, and positive relationships.

Unbalanced Chakra: Unhealthy relationship to one's sexuality, loss of innocence and wonder, loss of wonder regarding the magic of life. Self judgment, lack of healthy boundaries, blocked in self expression, suppresses needs and desires.

The Solar Plexus Chakra –
Our Center of Power

The solar plexus chakra receives and distributes energy throughout the physical form. This fire center, Manipura, meaning lustrous gem, our emotional and power center, is also called the sea of turmoil because of the stormy seas we endure on life's journey.

Modern society works through the solar plexus chakra. People are conditioned to fulfill desires, seek personal power and build a false self. To calm this center, affirm: "I have all I need and more, my power comes from the source."

Along with striving for personal power, the solar plexus chakra synthesizes and controls decision-making. Our transformation process makes us responsible for our true empowerment, which comes from listening to our intuition.

Under the influence of personal will and the personality, this chakra reflects a yellow color representing thought. When transcending the personal self and allowing true wisdom to come forth, this chakra reflects the gold of wisdom and abundance. The solar plexus is our guide to the world around us and provides an important protective force until our inner light becomes completely balanced. A balanced, open solar plexus chakra brings inner joy, surrender and lightness. Imbalance brings depression, hopelessness, separation and striving.

The solar plexus chakra governs impressions and discrimination. It repels, magnifies, and reflects the duality of thoughts and emotions. It is a connecting link to the mental and spiritual consciousness. The solar plexus receives information from the mental and higher mental and translates it through the chakras of the heart and throat. It also receives information from the physical and etheric fields and translates them through the root and navel chakras. This feeling center of the body picks up on the energy of others; it can be thought of as a transmitting tool, accessing information from all fields.

The energy of the solar plexus chakra is linked deeply with the heart. As we let go of our personal striving, the lotus of the solar plexus turns from pointing downward to pointing upward to the heart forming a bridge of light that assists the lower chakras to unite with the higher. A journey into our heart chakra is an experience of peace and calmness.

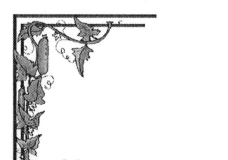

The
Solar Plexus
Chakra Chart

Manipura:
Meaning lustrous gem, city of gems

Location: The well between the shoulder blades (backside) in between the navel and sternum (front side)

Physical Correspondence: Digestive system (particularly liver and small intestine), muscles, stomach, gall bladder, nervous system, pancreas, lower back, physical solar plexus, endocrine glands

Physical Dysfunctions: Allergies, digestive problems, assimilation of energy, nervous disorders, fatigue, pain in middle and lower back

Subtle Body: Astral and emotional

Glandular Connection: Pancreas and adrenals-controls liver, digestive system, stomach, spleen, gall bladder, autonomic nervous system, lower back, muscles

Emotional Plane: Main emotion: Fear – false sense of power through wrong identification, low sense of self, need to be in control, manipulation, insecurity

Mental Plane: Letting go of unwanted thoughts and accumulation from the past, believing in your true nature, diving into the unknown essence of being, surrendering to the master in the heart. Relates to reasoning.

Color: Golden or yellow

Petals: 10

Element: Fire

Symbol: A ten-petaled lotus flower containing a downward-pointing triangle surrounded by three T-shaped swastikas, or Hindu symbol of fire.

Sense: Sight, shaping of being

Fragrance: Peppermint, lemon, rosemary, lavender, carnation, cinnamon, marigold, chamomile, thyme

Ayurvedic Oils: Sandalwood, lavender and fennel

Healing Stones: Citrine, turquoise, lapis, amber, tiger eye, topaz, aventurine, quartz

Sounds: Vowel C spoken in lower c

Mantra: RAM

Words to create healing affirmations: Power, source, divine will, becoming, honor, respect, discernment, receive, surrender, let go, peace, wholeness, purpose, meaning, self will, courage, inner strength

Verbs: I can, I am,

Yoga Postures: Bow Pose, Belly Push, The Woodchopper, Sun Salutation

Balanced Center: Feeling peace and harmony with inner self, actions are performed with a deep reverence for life; light and energy are your expressions. Living for the highest good for all concerned, wishes are fulfilled spontaneously because of the emission of light that you give.

Unbalanced Center: There is a mistaken identification of the false nature of the self driven by personal power. Power is used to manipulate life according to self-centeredness. There is a lack of genuine self-worth. Disturbance often due to emotions held deep within. Striving, positioning and aggression are expressions of a sense of low self-worth, as are fear of failure, unworthiness and using power for self-gain.

The Heart Chakra –
Our Wisdom Center

The fourth chakra, Anahata, is the source of all light and love. This is where the lower chakras and the higher chakras meet and become integrated, creating oneness of being. The heart center opening demonstrates the deepest action of love turned inward.

The heart is the meeting ground of the spiritual triad of love, will and wisdom. This meeting occurs when the head center becomes the point of contact for spiritual will, the heart center becomes the agent for spiritual love and the throat center becomes the expression of the spiritual mind.

The heart chakra functions to protect, heal and bring balance to the body, mind and emotions. Because this chakra is closely associated with the thymus gland, which governs the immune system, it is quite vulnerable to our overall level of health.

The heart chakra awakens us to the qualities of love, forgiveness and compassion helping to release the painful memories of the past. The heart chakra is a bridge of light between the lower centers and the higher. All must cross this bridge to move from the limited consciousness of personality to divine conscious-ness. The heart forgives, letting go of memories that bind us to the past. The forgiveness process opens the door to true compassion for our life and our relationships and creates the miracle of understanding, forgiving and ending the habit of blaming others for our situation.

The heart chakra opens when the personal will is transformed to divine will and personal power evolves to an empowered heart devoted to peace, giving and receiving love and the practice of discernment. Unconditional love, compassion towards others and ourselves replaces self-centered desire and want. Cherishing our sacred energy, we give from our overflow.

The heart center opens through surrender of our separate sense of self. The doorway leads us to meet our inner lord, our beloved guide. This sage within is with us through all life's experiences. Identification with our lower self obstructs our meeting with this inner teacher. Contact with our inner guide brings spiritual love, wisdom and will, in the rhythm of nature and according to divine law.

The
Heart Chakra
Chart

Anahata:
Meaning un-struck, pure, unbroken;
the love chakra.

Location: Heart, center of the chest

Physical Correspondence: Thymus, blood, life force, vagus nerve, circulation

Physical Dysfunctions: Heart disease, cancer, high blood pressure, breathing and circulation problems, immune system diseases, skin disorders

Subtle Body: Mental and higher mental

Glandular Connection: Thymus – controls heart, blood, circulation, immune system, lower lungs, rib cage, skin, upper back, and hands

Emotional Plane: Main emotion: Love – co-dependency, melancholia, loneliness, betrayal, devotion

Mental Plane: Love that is blocked by thought patterns and conditioning. Thoughts geared to conditional love based on ideas, things, bargains, comparison, the past.

Colors: Green – healing, pink – divine love

Petals: 12, inside of which are two overlapping triangles forming a six-pointed star, representing the ability of the individual to evolve upward or downward.

Element: Air

Symbol: Lotus of twelve petals, containing two intersecting circles that make up a six pointed star descending toward matter and pointing upward, raising matter toward spirit. Small chakra below heart called Ananakanda Lotus is the celestial wishing tree that holds the deepest wishes of the heart.

Animal Correspondence: Deer, gazelle, antelope

Sense: Touch

Fragrance: Attar of roses, bergamot, clary sage, geranium, rose

Ayurvedic Oils: Rose, lavender, sandalwood

Healing Stones: Rose quartz, tourmaline, kunzite, emerald, jade, watermelon tourmaline, azurite, aventurine quartz, malachite, moonstone

Sounds: Ay as in ray

Mantras: YAM

Words to create healing affirmations: Love, compassion, open, receive, accept, forgive, release, surrender, enjoy, joy, peace, harmlessness, unconditional, freedom, sacred, essence, being, honor, worthy, give

Verbs: I love, I accept, I forgive, I release, I am

Yoga Postures: Cobra, Fish, Windmill, Cow Head pose, Salutation to the Sun

Balanced Center: When this center is balanced, all centers are in harmony. There is a feeling of unconditional love, surrender of letting go to a higher will. Open to divine guidance. There is a radiance of love, sincerity, compassion and a deep feeling of wholeness.

Unbalanced Center: Love given from an unbalanced heart center has a conditional quality, expects something in return or recognition of some kind. It is difficult to accept love and support from others; we are not open to receive. Being sensitive and gentle are qualities that feel embarrassing and we build up a defensive mechanism.

The Illuminated Heart

Through the opening of the heart chakra we become spiritual warriors, protecting our sacred energy from the pitfalls of illusion and cultivating harmlessness. The symbol for the heart chakra is the deer. The gentle deer finds Ahimsa, the path of peace in daily life. Like the deer, the aspirant places his complete trust in God.

The heart center opening can be painful. It is the cross that we must bear when leaving our identification with the temporary nature of life. The heart chakra masters the polarities of the emotional, mental and etheric fields. The lower impulses of the chakras of the personality are transformed to reflect our true essence of divinity. Initiation into the heart chakra develops the qualities of reverence, service, compassion and selfless love.

With the gateway of the heart open, we sense a deeper presence within our lives, giving us the protection, devotion and strength needed for our journey home. Our journey takes us into our luminous body of light where we begin a life of service and devotion to the divine.

The song of the heart brings great love, beauty and unbounded joy. Our divine call on the path of return, this song is heard in the silence of the heart, teaching us about deep compassion and forgiveness – the healing miracles.

The Flowering Lotus of the Heart

The lotus of the heart is connected to the world through compassion; remaining untouched by all worldly experiences. This most sacred lotus is always flowering in the rhythm of our inner life, releasing the divine nectar of pure love in support of our true nature. Within the depth of our divine heart is a sacred resting place where we can retreat in silence, a reservoir of love, pure wisdom and divine guidance. As each petal unfolds, the chalice of life is filled with sacred essence and we journey deeper into the silence of the heart through greater and greater levels of awareness. We no longer strive to be on the path of spiritual awakening; we are the path.

Opening the Lotus of the Heart

The **first petal** unfolds when we meet our innermost self within the heart sanctuary and awareness turns from identification with the body to knowing our true self.

The **second petal** opens through realization that we are neither our emotions nor our mind. Our true nature is an expression of divinity, found in the heart of goodness, in alignment with inner truth.

The **third petal** unfolds when thinking is used for higher aspiration and the mind becomes silent. The mind dissolves into the sacred heart, a silent observer, thought transforms to intuition, perception and discernment.

The **fourth petal** opens when we release attachment to the things of this world. The knowledge obtained within our heart's unfolding lotus deepens our understanding of pure consciousness.

The **fifth petal** unfolds when we are firmly embedded in our true nature, demonstrating steadfastness, vigilance and uncompromising clarity.

The **sixth petal** unfolds when all that is not pure consciousness is burned in the sacred fire of our inner light.

The **seventh petal** opens when our inner being is adorned with all-inclusive love, harmlessness and devotion to the ever-present sacred self that resides in the spiritual heart.

The **eighth petal** opens as we directly perceive our true reality. The light of consciousness removes all doubt.

The **ninth petal** opens when there is deep and profound peace, the past is dissolved completely and true freedom has been realized.

The **tenth petal** opens when we fully live each sacred moment, awaiting life's call to service.

The **eleventh petal** opens when we experience the joy of our being and share it with others.

The **twelfth petal** opens when we walk the path of compassion.

The Throat Chakra –
The Chakra of Miracles

The journey of consciousness takes us through the limitations of the lower chakras into the higher centers of our true self. In the realm of the throat chakra, Visuddha, we have the opportunity to express the joy of pure being-ness through the voice. The throat center teaches us to use sound, prayer and affirmations for healing and balancing any discord of our body, mind and emotions. A beautiful blue light emanates from this center in various shades according to the vibration of our expression.

The lessons of the throat center teach the importance of honesty, discernment, listening and hearing, observing the voice of doubt, judgment, self-criticism and other untruths held deep within our conditioning. False perception of the self binds us to the conditioning of the past. The throat center is the bridge between the body and the mind, the connection between the feeling nature of our being and the higher wisdom of our sacred spirit.

As the throat chakra opens, we develop a clear expression of divine energies creating a link between the lower chakras and the upper chakras and ascend into the true essence, a new consciousness of willingness. Letting go of all habits, instincts and patterns of the ego that were based on preservation of the personality self, we now move into the expression of divine consciousness.

The highest expression of the Visuddha chakra is prayer – the deep communion between the true self and the higher omnipresent force of life. Prayer in this way is the process of ever-deepening devotion and surrender to the highest will of the divine. The throat center is where we take the path of surrender, turning our thoughts and attention inward to the silence of our true self.

When we are in touch with our true nature we receive the gift of manifestation, where our deepest wishes are expressed and affirmed and all self-doubt is removed. The throat chakra is the primary tool in healing and transformation, expressing the truth of our authentic self. In relationship to the health of an individual, it is connected to the thyroid and parathyroid glands, which metabolize the energy of the system. Expressing truth, we create an opening for the grace of healing to take place.

The Path of Silence

Silence is the unseen power of the throat center, the space in which the creative word is expressed. Silence heals all imbalances of the body, mind and spirit, realigning us with our inner truth. Silence is the avenue we must take in order to free ourselves from unwanted thought and disturbance that comes from identification with the changing nature of life. It is a great centering device, bringing coordination, order and calmness so that we may tap into our creative resources and co-create through our divine guidance. Through silence we build our vital force and keep it as a reservoir for our creative expression.

Silence stills our mind, emotions and bodily sensations allowing us to experience the peace of our heart and our witness consciousness. The voice of the silence within our heart is our divine guide and teacher, opening us to greater possibilities of self-understanding. Within silence, the intentional breath and the relaxation they bring, we enjoy a conscious communion with our source and keep the flame of our heart burning brightly.

The way to mastery is to turn within to the silence of the true self and live in stillness, unaffected by the changing appearances of manifestation in the eternal essence of life.

The
Throat Chakra
Chart

Visuddha:

Meaning purification, simplified,
sanctified, free from doubt.
The chakra of miracles.

Location: Between collarbones, third cervical vertebrae, base of neck

Physical Correspondence: Throat, neck, thyroid, parathyroid, ears, mouth, teeth

Physical Dysfunctions: Sore throats, colds, swollen glands, neck pain, dental
problems, thyroid problems, asthma, hearing or ear problems

Subtle Body: Buddhic

Glandular Connection: Thyroid and parathyroid—controls jaw, neck, throat, voice,
airways, upper lungs, nape of neck, arms

Emotional Plane: Inability to express emotions, blocked creativity, transformation
of feelings and emotions, communication, reflections

Mental Plane: Blocked flow of creative expression by thought and self-doubt;
thought and mind create negativity about self and block ability to express emotions; low self-esteem due to thought and conditioning

Color: Bright blue—expression; light blue—the quality of truth

Petals: 16

Element: Ether

Symbol: Lotus with 16 petals, containing a downward pointing triangle within a
circle representing the full moon

Animal Correspondence: Elephant holding one of his seven trunks up victori-
ously.

Sense: Hearing

Fragrance: Sage, eucalyptus, frankincense, lavender, sandalwood, chamomile,
myrrh

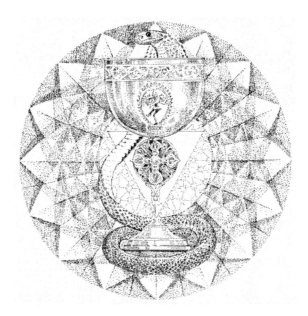

Ayurvedic Oils: Sandalwood, tea tree

Healing Stones: Aquamarine, turquoise, chalcedony, lapis lazuli, agate, celestite, sodalite, sapphire

Sounds: EEE

Mantra: HAM

Words to create healing affirmations: Express, self, listen, be truthful, voice, power, affirm, command, commune, allow, harmony in expression, harmlessness, wishes, invoke, prayer, communication, creative, ask, miracles, sanctify

Verbs: I speak, I bring forth, I ask, I allow, I open

Yoga Postures: Neck Rolls, Fish Pose, Shoulder Stand, The Plough, Head Lift, Salutation to the Sun

Balanced Chakra: We express our thoughts, feelings and emotions with inner knowing and without fear. We allow ourselves to be honest with others and ourselves. Speech is clear, reflecting inner truth. Silence is easily practiced.

Unbalanced Chakra: Sometimes we will express ourselves in thought-less actions or shut ourselves off from our feelings of truth. There is often a pattern of judgment of self and others. Voice can be abrasive, loud and offensive. Insufficient energy in the throat chakra can express itself in shyness, being overly quiet and getting a lump in the throat when needing to speak.

The Third Eye Chakra –
The Center of Perception

The third eye chakra is Ajna – Sanskrit for "to perceive the eye of wisdom" – the center of higher intuition. Our sixth sense, clairvoyance, is developed in the third eye chakra. The related endocrine gland is the pituitary gland, which is said to be the seat of the soul.

This sixth chakra gives will and the power of visualization. The master for all the other chakras, the opening of the Ajna is vitally important to achieving full potential in our lifetime. Quieting the mind, deep contemplation and inquiry into the nature of the true self are the paths to accomplishing this opening. This center, when fully awakened, has the power to transform all conditions of our life, releasing karmic patterns from the past and healing body, mind and emotions.

The third eye center, when awakened, illuminates our path with the radiant light of spirit and takes us to deeper levels of perception and balance where the energy of matter and spirit become one. Closing our outer eyes we find a deep peace within our inner eye. Meditation becomes a vehicle to rest in the light of our pure consciousness.

The saying, "Be in the world but not of it," is appropriate for the development of the ajna center as we learn to shift our attention from the world of change to the changeless essence of the divine.

The question, "Who am I?" leads us safely to the essence of our true self. The wisdom eye is the window to our radiant true nature and, when opened, it gives us insight to our divine purpose. This window reflects the light of the soul, the realm of our higher knowledge, and frees us to discover the eternal presence within our hearts.

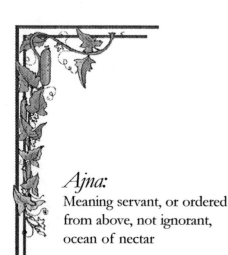

The
Third Eye
Chakra Chart

Ajna:
Meaning servant, or ordered
from above, not ignorant,
ocean of nectar

Location: First cervical vertebra, center of the head at the eye level or slightly above.

Physical Correspondence: Pituitary gland, left lower brain, left eye, ears, nose, nervous system

Physical Dysfunctions: Headaches, poor vision, eye problems, nightmares

Subtle Body: Intuitive

Glandular Connection: Pituitary, controls endocrine system

Emotional Plane: Lack of ability to integrate feelings with wisdom, learning difficulties, hallucinations. How we see determines our experience.

Mental Plane: Thoughts and conditioning, mind blocks clear perception

Spiritual Plane: Extrasensory perception, knowledge of being

Color: Indigo

Petals: Two, associated with hemispheres: left–analytical, logical, mathematical and linear; right–spatial, artistic, intuitive and holistic

Element: Ether, light and telepathic energy

Symbol: Lotus with 2 large petals on either side, resembling wings, around a circle containing a downward pointing triangle.

Sense: Sixth sense, light

Fragrance: Mint, jasmine, violet, rose, lotus, geranium, rosemary, basil

Ayurvedic Oils: Sandalwood, basil, lavender, jasmine, eucalyptus

Healing Stones: Lapis lazuli, blue sapphire, sodalite, quartz, opal

Sounds: Vowels, sound therapy vowel sound E sung in A

Mantra: KSHAM

Words to create healing affirmations: Understanding, harmony, oneness, knowing, intuition, light, seeing, awareness, vision, recognition, inner truth, trust, divine plan, imagination, visualization, clarity, purpose, willingness, servant, light

Verbs: I see, I am, I create, I ask, I command

Yoga Posture: Palming the eyes

Balanced Chakra: There is a developed level of perception, listening to one's inner voice. There is no longer a sense of duality, as this center, when fully awakened, expresses the middle path of equilibrium and the inherent unity of life. We attain the gift of visualization and the ability to comprehend life intuitively.

Unbalanced Chakra: Overly intellectual, critical and rational, lacks a holistic way of thinking, and an inability to integrate. We block the light of our vision with our conditioned thought. We sometimes are not able to integrate the experience that we have had in our changing life and lose perception of reality.

The Crown Chakra –
The Chakra of Unity

The crown chakra – Sahasrara, the thousandfold lotus – is located on the top of the head at the baby's soft spot. This exquisite white thousand-petaled lotus forms a most beautiful crown on the head with the stem or Antahkarana; the bridge of light between personality and soul; reaching upward as a channel for divine energies. It is the soul's point of entry and exit as well as a receiving and distributing station for our life force. It is most activated through yearning to unite with our inner true nature as well as the inquiry into the sacred nature of life.

Opening the crown chakra allows the divine to clear past impressions and to create an unconditional relationship to life based on the present. Jesus said, "Empty thyself and I shall fill thee," which implies a divine energy entering through the crown. When we empty ourselves of the scars and conditioning of the past we are born anew into the light.

The crown chakra is a center for universal consciousness with the duty of integrating and synthesizing all energies into one unified whole. The seventh chakra connects us with divine energy that purifies and unifies us with our life's purpose. The channel widens as our consciousness expands taking us deeper into our unknown mysterious nature.

Related to the pineal gland, the crown chakra holds the thread of consciousness that connects us with our soul. The seventh chakra is an organ of synthesis where the will, creativity and consciousness are integrated. It unifies the beauty of the heart center, the truth of the throat center and the goodness of the third eye center.

We develop a closer connection with our true self with each step of our ascension process. Opened through silence, purity and meditative prayer, this center moves down through the spinal column unifying, healing and balancing our body, mind and spirit. The centers along the spine come into full expression when all negative conditions are released.

The
Crown Chakra
Chart

Sahasrara:
Meaning granting victory,
possessing one thousand-petaled
lotus, or immortal self.

Location: Top and center of the head, the baby's soft spot

Soul Lesson: Unity, integration

Physical Correspondence: Pituitary, pineal gland, upper brain, right eye, central nervous system

Physical Dysfunctions: Immune system, circulation, endocrine disorders

Subtle Body: Divine

Glandular Connection: Pineal—controls cerebrum, right brain hemisphere, central nervous system, right eye

Emotional Plane: Depression, obsession, confusion, hopelessness, disassociation, ungrounded. When the seventh chakra is closed the accumulated wisdom and lessons of the soul remain unconscious. The open seventh chakra becomes the channel of communication to the higher self.

Mental Plane: The chatter of the mind becomes unbearable, psychotic, thoughts that create anxiety, frustration, and fear.

Colors: Gold, white or violet

Petals: 1000

Element: All elements, thought, cosmic energy

Symbol: A 1000-petaled lotus flower

Sense: Beyond self, thought

Fragrance: Lavender, frankincense, lotus, rosewood, spruce, olibanum

Ayurvedic Oils: Sandalwood, frankincense, myrrh

Healing stones: Amethyst, clear quartz, diamond, crystal, topaz, alexandrite, sapphire, selenite

Sound or Mantra: Om

Words to create healing affirmations: I am, universe, connections, spirit, channel, open, radiant, choose, transformed, release, surrender, open, contentment

Verb: I know, I am, I realize

Yoga postures: Half lotus, head stand, meditation

Balanced Center: We have journeyed from our expression as separate individuals and have integrated all our experiences and gifts, we live in deep surrender and acceptance of life as it is. Now we experience life as a divine inner child and remember the magical journey of our childlike nature. Through the development of this center we are balanced with our earth energies and can access our subconscious feelings.

Unbalanced Center: Self Realization is a challenge as our thoughts and emotions are identified with our false sense of self. It is difficult to let go of our past experiences or integrate them, understanding the lessons we have learned. We often experience depression and feel out of touch with life.

The Art of Meditation

Meditation is a state of communion with the divine, the pure essence of God within our heart. True meditation begins when we know ourselves as a spark of the divine source. The knowledge of our true self gives us the inner strength and courage to live in a way that honors our purpose in life.

As the mind dissolves into the heart of stillness, the divine in all of creation becomes visible. No longer a separate self, believing in our thoughts as essential truth, we experience a unity in life. All is laid to rest in the peace of the sacred quiet mind. This force will guide, inspire, encourage and bring a positive energy to whatever we need. We cherish this light, this precious force, quietly abiding in its presence, ever faithful to the holy energy encountered.

This is how I would die into the love I have for you.
As pieces of clouds dissolve into sunlight.
Rumi

Chapter Five:

The Emotional, Mental or Spiritual Causes of Imbalances

The mind turned inward is the self;
turned outward, it becomes the ego
and all the world.

Nisargadatta Maharaj, I Am That

Many kinds of imbalances can occur in the energy fields. When the energy fields are working in harmony with each other under the direction of the soul, the vital force is strong. When, on the other hand, one of the fields such as the emotional field or mental field is not in agreement with the intention for healing and wholeness, it hampers the achievement of long lasting results and optimal health.

The etheric field functions to protect us from toxic debris of a physical, emotional or mental origin. To prevent imbalances from entering the system, this web around the physical must remain intact, strong and impenetrable. If weakened by toxins or emotional or mental stress, it allows a vulnerability to negative energy that often results in a breakdown of our system. Keeping our energy strong requires developing an awareness of our spirit nature and listening to its guidance. Our lives can be very fragile; at times we weaken under outside stresses and are damaged by memories of the past. As we identify with life's passing sorrows, our soul light withdraws and we lose vitality and optimism. This drains emotional energy, leaving the physical body susceptible to illness and creating confusion in our mental field. To effectively regain and maintain health we must learn to revitalize our soul force and call our fragmented selves back to the present moment. This requires breathing in vital energy, surrendering our hold on the past (good or bad) and re-energizing our life goals. The physical body guides us to listen to warning signs such as fatigue or pain, the emotional body asks us to transform and release unresolved emotions and the mental body calls us to renew our sense of self through the release of our conditioning and self-limiting belief systems. Healing the vital force requires that all aspects of our energy being be in alignment with the light of our soul.

Learning to be responsible for our energy field health, we can understand the cause of energy imbalance and apply the appropriate technique for healing and alignment. When looking for the cause of an imbalance we must look to all areas of the body-mind. For example, when our physical body is experiencing symptoms, we must not only observe our physical condition but look to the emotional and mental component to discover the causative factors. The art of observing our whole being is the key to long lasting healing.

Most imbalances stem from carrying frozen traumatic memories in our energy fields. Through developing awareness we learn to observe how our wounded past is repeated in our lives. We often attract relationships that have the same factors as those that originally damaged us. These repetitions have much to teach us. It is also possible to see our life patterns manifesting through our children, our work and all aspects of life. Our patterns can often be traced back into the roots of our existence creating a map by which we can transform our lives. These roots are tied to the conditioning of our ancestors. It is possible to heal all patterns of illness and conditioning by seeing the original error in misidentification. Awareness can lead us to freedom of being and return us to the wholeness of our authentic self. When we deepen our heart's compassion and begin the healing process in our life, it will radiate light to our relationships and our family and will act as preventative medicine for our future. The miracle of life is that we have the ability to instantly transform unresolved emotions from the past by seeing their core cause. Although the past may hold stories of untold suffering, we can bring these stories into a new light and reframe them by learning what gifts they have brought to us. Like the fertile ground of our gardens, the events of our past experiences can be used beautifully to prepare our life for new and positive growth.

Intentional Evolution

Most humans are searching for happiness, a search that often is fulfilled when a connection is made to our soul's purpose and discovery of our path of joy. When you set out to follow your joy, you tap into the secret chamber of the heart, the celestial wishing tree that holds the deepest desires of the heart. The heart's aspiration is the guiding light of your path. The saying "follow your heart" is so very true when it comes to being healthy, happy and holy on all levels. Physical, mental and emotional health are all linked to this path and many times it is not until this heart's path and desire is revealed that one is finally able to achieve health and well-being. This is demonstrated in an accelerated manner when a person hits bottom and then makes a breakthrough that shifts their identity, their mode of life and even their spiritual attunement, allowing them to make a miraculous recovery.

Our life force moves through phases of soul lessons that offer the opportunity to open to receive and deepen our wisdom. Each chakra that opens and is transformed brings more soul energy and a greater possibility of a vital life.

Becoming aware of unhealthy and healthy patterns, we observe the part of ourselves that wants to move ahead or rise upward, wants to say "yes" to life. At the same time we also see the part that does not move, or says "no" to life. Often a crisis develops because of these opposing forces and within this crisis, illness can take root. Some aspects of our being are magnetically attracted to the downward spiral of life. Fortunately these aspects can be trained to move upward with the aspect of our being that yearns to evolve in consciousness.

Energy healing discovers the root cause of an imbalance by using kinesiology to access the etheric, emotional, mental and spiritual energy fields. Learning to access the source of all healing and direct it to the energy field requires attention. If we need to forgive something in our past, we can access the healing light for assistance in the forgiveness process. If we need to change a certain belief or mental conditioning, we can create a new life affirmation or living prayer and energize it with our healing light. Understanding the healing process is simple but requires receptivity to the healing force. The healing light is supported by prayer, humility, and a willingness to receive.

We are Vibrational Beings

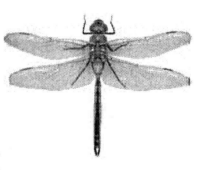

Everything is energy. We are energy beings that bring in and discharge energy in the great recycling system called Life. Our energy flows as part of the natural process of life, from observing nature and learning from her rhythms. Nature teaches us how to release, how to die, how to be reborn, how to blossom in beauty and how to let go again. It teaches us about stillness, movement, energy, light, dark, cold and hot. It teaches us about fire, wind, earth and water. These elements all reside in our body and express themselves energetically. Nature always leads us back to a feeling of equilibrium and calm. Because we are energy beings, we have the opportunity to see with our sixth sense and trust that inner vision. We can also learn to see where we need energy protection and to ward off negative forces.

Our delicate etheric energies need protection from illness producing forces. Though in time we are all subject to the simple processes of life, we can become the caretaker of our souls and work with our energy fields to create harmony, peace, good will and service in this lifetime. Saying "yes" to life means saying "yes" to good health, to positive thoughts and positive emotions. Saying yes means eliminating fear and negative thinking from our energy fields. We all have access to a great method to attain energy wellness, the source of all healing. The source is accessed through our willingness to receive our prayers, our breath, and great humility. Breathing healing light into our energy fields opens the path to the miracle of life itself. This source, when consciously applied to any area of imbalance, brings us the miracle of healing.

The Art of Energy Balancing

A current of electromagnetic energy travels through our body, mind and spirit, giving us our life direction, life essence and life vitality. When energy is in balance there is a free flow of our life essence. Each energy field functions optimally at a balanced frequency, an energy equilibrium. With energy balanced in the etheric, emotional, mental and spiritual energy fields, health follows. The frequency at which we resonate depends upon how we function on the etheric, emotional, mental and spiritual fields.

The Etheric Energy Field – Keys to Abundant Energy

The etheric blueprint duplicates the physical body and when weakened shows signs of stress. Etheric energy imbalances are a result of stress on some level; of ignoring warning signs such as fatigue, loss of energy, depression and pain. When we listen to the body we can detect imbalances before they manifest as illness. We can learn to sense our internal messages and follow what the body is requiring for its sustenance. When the body speaks to us in the form of pain or discomfort, we become its most cherished caretaker. Honoring its messages and yielding to its direction brings balance to all aspects of our being. Through this listening we learn to apply the healing force of love to our life, observing the root cause of the imbalance. For this we must be honest about our thinking habits, our emotional expressions and our connection with nature and the divine in life. If we are diligent we can usually trace a physical symptom back to an emotional experience or a time of negative thinking. We can also observe when life is calling for communion with nature and the silence of our divine self.

Our life essence enters through the chakras, and then flows into the nadis and meridians, nourishing the energy fields. Since the etheric energy is the blueprint of the physical it is important to keep it strong and free from disturbances and energy blocks.

The etheric field is a bridge that relays information from the emotional and mental fields to the physical. Any emotional disturbance is very likely to impose some level of stress or pain on the body. If there is continual unresolved emotional or mental field disturbance it can eventually create disease in the physical body. The universal energy functions as life breath or Prana is received and distributed through the body. When Prana or life breath is distributed freely throughout the etheric and released freely, the energy fields stay in harmony and balance.

The Emotional Field – Keys to Emotional Well Being

In the emotional field, imbalances usually begin during periods of emotional stress when we are not allowing emotions to flow through and out of the body. When anger, for example, is suppressed time and time again, it often turns into depression, which can lead to a weakened system. On the other hand, continuous expression of strong anger can break down the internal organs and open the body to disease and disharmony. Healthy anger is merely a call to speak our truth at the appropriate moment with ease and honesty, but anger that is rooted in fear is a reflection of our disharmony with divine energies. Transcend this kind of anger by increasing the vibration of love.

Emotions are a gift to understand others and ourselves. From them we learn the art of listening to the voice of the heart. This requires energy and freedom from past emotions that color our experience of life in the now. When emotions accumulate from the past they become lodged in the aura, waiting for new experiences to assist in their release. Because of these past emotions it becomes difficult to live in the now. To be well emotionally we must learn to let go, die to the past and release all past trauma. This means we must consciously surrender our attachment to memory, give all to the sacred fire of life and begin to fully live in the present.

The Mental Field – Keys to Mental Well Being

In the mental field, imbalances begin when the mind is not used constructively. The mind is like a piece of clay and needs to be molded and refined to become the most useful tool. When the mind is not directed properly, it is open to negative thinking habits that can result in illness and disharmony. The mind, when quiet, can be an instrument of beauty, perceiving spiritual truths of the universe. Through the quiet mind we have access to our higher nature which holds the healing light of love, wisdom and compassion. The mind, when allowed to run unguided, expresses thoughts of a lower nature, directing the emotional level to anger, greed, desire, attachment, fear, envy and so forth. When

*To spirit, getting is meaningless
and giving is all.*
T,67 – A Course in Miracles

the mind is used as a witnessing tool, it is of great service on our journey, assisting us to stay centered, still and well balanced through life's changes. When the mind is mastered, unwanted thoughts no longer dictate our actions and the attention turns from outward things back to the silence of the heart.

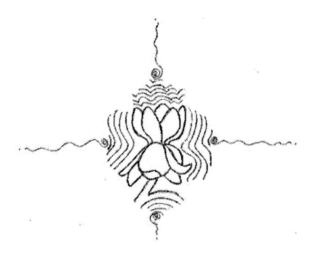

The Web of Mind and Emotions

The inner energy fields of the etheric, emotional, mental and spiritual bodies radiate out in the aura like a spectrum of rainbow light. When the energy is free from disturbances, the aura is luminous with light, beauty and aspiration. The school of life brings many tests and lessons so you can grow into your full potential as a Light Being. Awakening to your true potential invites you to let go of areas in your life that hold a false sense of self through misidentification. You realize that you are not just your body, mind and emotions, and begin the search for deeper answers as to the nature of your true self.

Your emotions and thoughts influence your energy frequency. When you feel and think in ways that support your health and well being, your energy frequency vibrates at a higher level. When you feel and think in ways that are not supportive to your health and well being, your frequency is at a lower level. The conscious raising of your vibration serves to maintain your health on all levels.

In Eastern teachings, Kama-Manasic is the word used to describe the web of mind and emotions. When there are unresolved emotional and mental patterns, it becomes frozen energy in the field, creating a web that is often difficult to overcome. This frozen energy produces a deficiency in the flow of your life force and eventually could affect your health.

Unveiling What You Are Not – Recovering What You Are

Wouldn't it be refreshing to just feel brand new, unburdened by impressions and memories of the past? Your life is a flower; and your true essence is within the core of your flower. Each petal represents your experience in life. The true essence of you is found in the core.

Life can be understood as a long journey in which you start out with an empty suitcase and through time the suitcase becomes full of the content of your experiences. These experiences form your identity as a personality but deep inside there is something alive that is not effected or changed through your experiences. This first step in awakening is to realize you cannot be defined through the accumulations of your experiences, your image, or through any means found in the outer world.

Throughout your life there are many tests and lessons, or cause and effect, which are your karmic condition. The condition of your karma directly relates to your actions from the past; each action plants a seed of a new life possibility. That is why it is most important to see your life as a karma bank account, where you invest the right energy for the right results. Each lesson of your karmic condition offers you the choice to let go of aspects of your being that are no longer functioning for your higher good. Each lesson holds a hidden gift in the transformation process that aligns you with your higher purpose such as living in truth, compassion, and awareness. Your path of awakening guides you to release obstacles to your inner gifts and reclaim your birthright of freedom.

Looking inward leads you to the realization that your sense of self is not confined or defined by your identification with body, mind, or emotions. The deeper you inquire about what you are not the closer you come to meeting your authentic self. As you surrender to what is no longer true, you embark upon the mysterious, sacred path of life.

Your precious life is an opportunity to live in awakening communion with the source of your life, opening, flowering and meeting the truth of your being. Realizing that you can no longer define who you are through any conditioning, you seek to open the door to the eternal flow of life.

What is not love is always fear,
and nothing else.
          T,302 – A Course in Miracles

Your path leads you to the inner chamber of your heart, where you hold the compassion and forgiveness for your errors that were born in ignorance. Your scripts, your story and the stories of others and all your relationships around the stories are released and you take a deep breath of freedom and well being. In this very moment you can see that the story cannot thrive without the belief in it and all of its contents. So, you begin the process of embracing the truth of yourself now, releasing your past and truly loving the freshness and newness of your most precious life.

Your true joy comes through the simple path of letting go, welcoming the flowering of your soul. This miraculous opening occurs when you journey to the unknown places of your being, the spaces that are free from the content of the past and the accumulated identification with false images of the self.

Transformation of Spiritual Fear into Spiritual Love

Your life intentions and goals create a path of ascension or upward striving through seeing and knowing your true purpose in life. Your true purpose is to evolve in love.

Through working with a life goal or healing intention the focus is on co-creating with life the true desires of your heart. To begin the healing process there must be a calming of thoughts that project into the future, and an establishment of faith in divine grace. The action of trusting in divine grace makes it possible to eliminate fear from the body.

Fear is twofold; one aspect comes from imminent danger, a natural warning to yield, or make the changes necessary for survival or protection. The second aspect, spiritual fear, stems from feeling separate from the source of love, a feeling of going against the stream of life. The emotion of fear is held in the body in the form of memories, shocks, and losses, suffering and personal tragedy. Life is full of painful memories, a sense of victim consciousness and endless searching for the reasons things have happened the way they have.

Facing the Shadow Self

The shadow aspect of our energy field, also called here the Energy Culprit, often expresses through resisting right or corrective action of the moment. This is the part of us that holds back in subtle disagreement with our intention for healing and wholeness. The deeper the conflict between that part of us that is unaware and drawn to perpetuating suffering, and the part of us that has the intention to evolve, the more spiritual crisis we might experience. The ascension toward the light requires that we let go of our baggage so we can travel freely without heavy burdens. The ascension process takes us deep into the heart where our sacred presence heals all sense of separation. The shadow part of us creates suffering from holding onto a separate sense of self that has its roots in the past. When we begin to take responsibility for the light of our being, we simply bring the shadow into the light. With great compassion, the negative and self-limiting aspects of the shadow are infused with this great healing light.

Only you can deprive yourself of anything.
Do not oppose this realization
for it is truly the beginning
of the dawn of light.
T,186 – A Course in Miracles

Chakras often hold unresolved emotions or belief systems that prevent you from realizing your true nature. Each chakra holds the potential of divine flowering and the seeds of suffering that keep you from this flowering.

The *Root Chakra* holds the shadow aspect of our being that relates to unresolved fears, family, ancestral karma and security issues.

The *Navel Chakra* holds the shadow aspect of our being that relates to our sense of self, our feelings of shame, relationships, finances and physical creativity.

The *Solar Plexus* Chakra holds the shadow aspect of our self regarding our power issues, our judgment and opinions, our self-esteem and taking responsibility for our self.

The *Heart Chakra* holds the shadow aspect of us regarding over-concern for others, codependency, lack of self-love and lack of compassion and deep feelings of loneliness.

The *Throat Chakra* holds the shadow aspect of self regarding our inability to tell the truth, our lack of silence, and how we express truth and the right use of will.

The *Third Eye Chakra* holds the essence of the shadow in our inability to perceive things, thinking in terms of duality and our lack of inner vision and trusting in our intuition.

The *Crown Chakra* holds the shadow aspect in our inability to integrate life experiences and bring the energy from each chakra up to a higher vibration. The crown chakra also reflects our ability to receive divine grace, release our inner obstacles and open to our God-Self.

Conscious Choices and Healing Intentions

The foundation in which we dream, live our life and believe in our life comes from our inner sense of self. We have the choice in the essence of life, to dream consciously, creating dreams that offer the most happiness and peace to our world. Our self-esteem is perhaps the most important area of our life to nurture and protect, as it is the ground of being from which all acts spring. We have the choice to return to our original authentic self and discover what life means to us, without the conditioning of the past. The core conditioning and programming that creates self-limiting beliefs and emotional responses stem from our sense of unworthiness that is rooted in our past conditioning. This core programming is released through conscious choice and healing intentions.

To begin our life healing and transformation process, we must reconstruct the ground of our being. Breathing in, we reaffirm that life is safe, abundant, and secure and all our needs are met. We teach our inner precious being to believe and trust in the goodness of life, the flowering of life. We see that our inner garden of spiritual gifts is full of living potentials and we become a willing participant in letting go of ideas, concepts, beliefs, and conditioning that are not in harmony with our inner flowering.

The path of life teaches us how to trust in our self. We learn from the ascending path that life brings many lessons. This inner classroom teaches us to witness the roots of our sorrow, see the lessons, receive the gifts and release the energy of the lesson for the higher good. The energy culprit, as discussed previously, is the part of us that is not in agreement with the power we have to create our own reality of positive energy and abundance.

When we pay attention to the energy culprit, the self-defeating part of our life, we increase its power. We learn to create the life we want from believing in the fullness of life, not the lack. Each moment is an opportunity to live responsibly toward our soul and learn to respond to the teachings of the moment, living according to its divine messages. Daily we are given the opportunity to meet the challenges of our self-limiting belief systems and open ourselves to our endless opportunity to co-create with this most blessed universe.

Our life path offers glimpses of our joy, what truly brings happiness and peace. Opening, surrendering and reaching for our potential, we may find our greatest joy in service to others who are suffering. Being true to our inner self is perhaps the most important part of service, for it helps others in finding and being true to their path. This truth is the raising of consciousness into the light, for the good of all concerned and the fruits are unconditional joy.

Living with clear intentions and healing aspirations allows the energy to focus in a channel of ascension, a path in which to travel through all the obstacles to reach our full potential. When the mind and emotions are in harmony and reaching for a higher good or our soul's purpose, the universe supports this evolution of love. When self-limiting thoughts, fear and self-centered desires are at the root of our life intention, the universe vibrates at a much lower frequency. This creates a display of self-limiting experiences in our life that reflect our fear based thinking. Thoughts and emotions directed toward upholding and striving for goodness, beauty and light create higher frequencies that allow for divine action in our life.

The soul holds the truest and deepest desires of our heart. These are usually spiritual aspirations that reflect the light of our soul, and are the foundation in which life manifests. Creating a life goal comes from the foundation that you believe you can reach and attain your full potential, a positive attitude being the first building block.

Through seeing that the highest good is always manifesting in our life, we can reconnect with our sense of trust and affirm that there has always been a presence operating and witnessing our life. Paying attention to our inner being is most essential, seeing the pure witness consciousness that has been present throughout all our life changes. Deep inside we embrace and commune with the eternal unchanging aspect of our being. We connect the threads of our life and see a most beautiful tapestry of love and protection, affirming there is a reason for everything.

The mind of light generates thoughts that support the upward movement of the soul evolving in love. All thoughts bear seeds that burrow into our energy fields and are fed by emotions and the belief in them, and then reinforced by further thinking. Most self-defeating thoughts have their roots in fear and need to be infused with the light of spiritual energy. We must reestablish our faith in our life purpose, a soul goal, healing intention, or conscious choice. Then we embrace the energy culprit, the part of us that is in a state of fear and release it to the greater light of our true nature.

The creative force of our evolving soul is empowered through willingness to let it go and let it flow in our lives. We must not be afraid of our inner power to create and manifest life in our fullest visions. We must take the steps needed to let go of self-limiting beliefs that stem from conditioning and embedded patterns. Belief in the unlimited possibilities of being is vital to the path of true empowerment. The core ingredient for manifesting a life of joy, light and abundance is clear intention and the ability to release obstacles to this intention.

The Light of the Soul

Our highest potential can be discovered in the intuitive plane as we reach beyond the confines of our rational mind into the unknown, mysterious aspects of our being. The ajna or third eye chakra, the center of perception, opens through the evolution of the intuitive plane. An awakened intuitive field gives clear, perceptive thinking that stems from our soul energy. Personality linked with soul expresses true unity and harmony. This integration uses personality as a vehicle for our soul to follow the will of the higher good.

As discussed previously, the Kama-Manasic personality is a web of mind and desire, which brings many challenges to our life. When our desires and thoughts are stilled, we hear the voice of our soul and can surrender to its sacred guidance.

The causal field or soul level holds the essence of our true nature and endures all we experience along our path of evolution. This celestial energy field is also known as the Karana Sharia, meaning plane of cause and effect or karma. This plane holds the essence of the seeds of goodness that are extracted from our life experiences.

This plane of consciousness or seed body holds the energy for manifesting our deepest soul desires, aligned for the higher good for all concerned. The focus of thought or idea with attention manifests the secret of our soul power. On this plane the higher mental is expressed through blending mind and love, as wisdom. The spiritual energy field holds the essence of our soul's evolution in love. Uniting the energy of spirit and matter enhances the power of our soul.

The evolving energy of our personality travels through the tests of the chakras, passing through initiations into higher levels of consciousness. The correct use of will develops the solar plexus chakra and the surrender of our personal power. This surrender opens the gateway of our heart where the power of presence awakens to become our inner guide, leading us to purity of mind and the ability to truly love. This guide teaches us to discern unreal or false aspects of life and to know the real and true aspects. We are lead to the realization that we truly are a light being.

The heart center is related to either the higher or lower mental energy field. When it is related to our lower mental energy field, it functions through self-centered love that is limited and geared toward selfishness. Our higher mental energy field expresses impersonal love that acts unselfishly and unconditionally. The heart chakra when awakened transcends the personal seeds of suffering and lives in harmlessness of body, mind and soul. The sacred presence within our heart asks us to release the past and be reborn into the light of our true reality. This inner chamber purifies, awakens and brings peace to our new life.

Harmlessness in word, deed and action are the qualities of our new found being where we no longer can live in the consciousness of personality self. We return the mind to the silence of our heart and dissolve all sense of separation. Our hearts beat to a new rhythm, one that is in harmony with our higher calling, the inner beat of the master.

The Heart Initiation is the first initiation of the disciple of truth and it is at this time in the evolution of our soul that we take the *Path of the Lighted Way*. The opening of the heart center awakens the sacred presence within that holds our hand on our journey home. Life changes deeply from living of the world with worldly pursuits, to living in the world but not of it, knowing it is a temporary stopover for our traveling souls. Our awakening is supported through our practice of meditation, contemplation, spiritual study and right perception. The foundation of our evolving soul enriches us with the divine qualities of love, wisdom and spiritual will.

Seek not perfume of a single heart
Nor dwell in its easeful comfort;
For therein abides
The fear of loneliness.
I wept
For I saw
The loneliness of a single love
In the dancing shadows
Lay a withered flower
The worship of many in the one
Leads to sorrow.
But the love of one in the many
Is everlasting bliss.

J. Krishnamurti
From Darkness to Light

The lower vehicles of our personality have been of great service, bringing us to the clear reality of our soul's purpose. We embrace our body, mind and emotions by infusing them with the light of our soul. Our mental body expresses the light through intelligence; our emotional body expresses the light through love and compassion. The spiritual will is the highest aspect of the soul and is the force that guides the lower vehicles in the unification process.

The light of our soul removes the false layers of the personality aspect of our being. This light must be cherished as a sacred possession. We learn to sustain our light by keeping it burning bright through the trials of worldly life. This luminous light is the conscious building block of our inner temple and must be held as a most precious jewel. The light of our soul makes contact through a silent mind and energizes our spiritual will to evolve in consciousness. When our mind, emotions, and soul are in harmony they unite in service to the Brotherhood of Light. This is the collective consciousness that holds the positive intention for unity, harmony and peace for all of mankind.

Let go of your attachment to the unreal and the real will swiftly and smoothly step into its own. Stop imagining yourself as being or doing this or that and the realization that you are the source and heart of all will dawn upon you. With this will come great love, which is not choice or predication, nor attachment, but a power which makes all things love-worthy and lovable.

Nisargadatta Maharaj, **I Am That**

Opening the Lotus of Our Soul

Within our sacred heart is an ever-unfolding divine lotus. Each petal of the lotus represents a moral development that allows the inner nectar to flow. These petals are expressions of our unfolding soul, the eternal timeless blossoming of life. Through the process of birth and death our evolution gradually unfolds along the many stages of individualization or initiation.

Meeting our true nature, turning the attention inward to the ever-present love within, we can stop the wheel of cause and effect. In this turning, we must remain devoted to our innermost source of power, the very center of our being.

We have within our reach a current of consciousness that flows from our soul down through the various subtle bodies into our personality consciousness. It is through the strengthening of our soul, alignment with God, and devotion to freedom that the bridge of light (antahkarana) to our higher nature is built.

The personality has within its nature desires that are not in harmony with Self-Realization or God Consciousness. The channel between the personality and the higher consciousness of man must be purified to allow the continuous inflow of divine energy, which brings the gifts of wisdom, power and love. We must recognize that our lower vehicles, which are based on survival, reproduction, desires, self-importance, fear, anger and greed, have directed our way of thinking in an uncontrolled and chaotic manner.

Samskaras are scars from our previous lives, creating negative patterns within our subconscious that often dictate the way we feel and think in our present day life. It is through realignment with our inner god force that we begin the mastery process of our lower bodies.

To begin this most sacred process of meeting our true nature we must learn the art of looking inward, gradually increasing our divine power and self-control. Meditation, the art of quieting the mind and the emotions, can assist in this effort, opening the channel for our soul to pour forth its essence and the personality becomes absorbed in divine consciousness.

Purification of our lower nature opens the channel so that divine energy and soul essence can travel freely through the crown chakra, permeating all aspects of our being. The energy fields of the physical, the emotional and the mental must become willing instruments of the higher self.

One way of becoming an instrument of the higher self is to observe when tendencies are not conducive to this state. Developing our inner consciousness and connection with our divine truth decreases the impact of the emotional and mental bodies. Through deeper awareness of our true nature we begin to discern between that which is temporary and pleasing to the personal self and that which is pleasing to the higher self, which brings more permanent joy and deepening awareness of our true nature.

The pure consciousness of the divine is, in reality, the consciousness of all beings veiled by the workings of the personal self. The more we realize our true essence, the less we are bound to the aspects of the personal self. When full realization and unity occur, we become whole and radiant beings.

The one wholly true thought
one can hold about the past
is that it is not here.

W,13 – A Course in Miracles

Chapter Six:

Energy Testing —
The Art of Kinesiology

Suffering is due to non-acceptance.
Nisargadatta Maharaj, **I Am That**

The Background of Kinesiology

The word Kinesiology comes from the Greek word kinesis, which means movement. Applied Kinesiology was developed by a chiropractor, Dr. George Goodheart in 1964. His discovery was based on the premise that body language never lies. Muscles in the body can be used as indicators of body language; a diagnostic art to inquire about the state of health chemically, structurally, ethereally, emotionally, mentally or spiritually. This assessment procedure was christened Applied Kinesiology, commonly called muscle testing. There are several branches of Applied Kinesiology; the Life Essence Awakening Process, (LEAP) focuses on one that has impacted many lay people and professional healers, Touch for Health.

Dr. John Thie, president of the International College of Applied Kinesiology founded by Dr. George Goodheart, began giving his patients self-care work to do at home. This work made such an impact on people's health that Dr. Thie wrote a book for lay people and health practitioners to use with their clients. That book, *Touch for Health*, has gained worldwide recognition and become a health care practice that offers preventative health maintenance and in-depth balancing procedures for optimal well being.

About Energy Testing

Energy Testing is a valuable biofeedback tool that offers insights into etheric, emotional, mental and spiritual questions. Energy Testing asks questions in which the body's response indicates a yes or no answer. The test offers a way to dialogue with the patterns of the energy fields and how to change the frequency of the patterns to raise the life essence. If the muscle tested is strong the energy test is saying, "I am doing fine, thank you." If it is weak it says so or, in effect, gives permission to analyze a certain area. When the correction or balance is offered and the muscle tests strong, then the body is answering, "This is what I needed." A muscle that is still weak is saying: "Let's investigate further." Energy Testing offers a key in which to find out information, and also ways to dialogue with the intuitive part of us. Follow the guidelines for Energy Testing until you feel confident about testing muscles.

Attunement: Opening the Healing Channel

It is very important at the beginning of each session to take the time to slow down, breathe consciously together, call in assistance from our higher guidance and ask that all the information received and progress made in the session be for the highest good. You can invite in your own and the client's spirit guides by name, as well as God, Great Spirit, The Mother, or any name by which you or the client wishes to address the higher power. Create your own spontaneous prayer, or invocation, or use something like the following:

"Together we breathe in the oneness and allow the light, sound and vibration of this divine presence to protect us and assist us in bringing through the highest good and the highest possible healing here and now."

Kinesiology Guidelines

Hydration

The electromagnetic system is very sensitive and requires sufficient hydration for effective function. Before testing, have the subject drink a small glass of water. Test for hydration using the Pinch Test. Hold a small piece of hair at the nape of the neck and at the same time test the arm muscle as described in the following paragraphs. If the test is weak water is needed. Offer water, and then test again. If the test is strong, then water is not needed.

Setup

Have the client either sit or lie on a treatment table. Make sure they are comfortable and check on any neck, shoulder or arm injuries, or pain that might have an effect on testing of their arm. Remove watches, rings, and other metal or electronic things from pockets, etc.

Indicator Muscles

Begin by choosing a muscle to test. For simplicity, we will use the deltoid or pectoral muscle.

Pectoralis Major Clavicular

Put arm out at a 90-degree angle at chest level. Look for a yes or no answer. The message is in the lock and within two seconds. Remember to test lightly, gently, slowly. Apply enough slow, gentle pressure so that you can feel whether the response holds firm or weakens in response to your question.

Deltoid Muscle Test

To test the body using the deltoid muscle the subject
holds their arm out to the side with the palm facing
the floor. The tester pushes straight down on the
forearm near the wrist with a smooth, light pressure.
Be sure that the pressure is applied above the wrist,
toward the elbow, so that there is no tendency to
bend the wrist. Two inches of movement are all that
is necessary to indicate a weak muscle. Do not push
the arm all the way down. Apply light pressure
downward and out to the side.

Yes and No Answers

When the muscle is strong it locks in within two
seconds and two inches. This indicates a yes answer.
When the muscle is weak it does not lock in within two
inches or two seconds; this indicates a no answer.

Lightness is the Key to Accuracy!

Use light pressure. Using two fingers above the wrist, test until the muscle locks
in, generally within two seconds. Apply gradual pressure even when testing
lightly. Do not overpower the subject. This is not a test of muscle strength or a
competition of forces. A muscle is locked if it does not move when tested within
the two second, two inch rule. The subject remains in a relaxed posture. Both
subject and tester breathe consciously.

Fine-tuning Your Muscle Testing – The Rule of Two

Two fingers – this means the pressure is light enough to do a muscle test with
two fingers and you feel it lock in or remain strong.

Two inches – If your arm moves more than about two inches we say that it is
switched off, or weak. Eventually, you will be able to feel a switched off muscle
with less movement.

Two seconds – This is long enough to apply the gradual increase in pressure and
to feel for the switched-on locking in effect.

Muscle Strength Clarification Sample Tests

"I am _____ (correct name, test) (incorrect name, test) now."

"I am 100% well on all levels." When the body goes weak in response to this statement, it is indicating that the statement is not true for the subject. In most cases this is a confirmation that the testing is working, as so few people are 100% well on all levels.

"The sky is purple," "My name is Sigmund Freud," "I am a bird," etc. When these test negative, again it is a confirmation that testing is working.

Check for Permission

IMPORTANT: At the beginning of any muscle testing session always ask your client for permission to test. You can ask for a verbal answer and muscle test for the answer as well.

Test for Clarity and Switching

Sometimes the bioelectric or neurological circuits in the body become reversed or switched. One can test for this situation in the following two ways:

a. State: "This system is clear for testing." Check yes/no. When the answer is no it means the energy system is switched off and needs to be cleared.

b. Bridge test: Place your fingertip between the client's eyebrows. Muscle test the arm. Then place the same finger, with the nail against the skin, at the same location. Muscle test again. If results are the same, either both strong or both weak, then the energy system is switched and needs to be cleared. If one test is strong, the other weak, they are not crossed and you are ready to proceed.

Clearing Techniques

Use any or all of the following clearing techniques until a recheck tests clear.

a. Rub K27 and the navel (see diagram, next page). On the chest, two inches below sternum feel for a hollow, an area that is usually tender to the touch.

b. Do the figure eight sweep and cross crawl as shown in the diagrams on following pages.

c. Rub the upper lip and lower lip.

d. Do sweeping figure eight motions around the body.

e. Eyes follow circle.

f. Tap Thymus.

g. Move hand up the central meridian from pubic bone to lower lip. Test.

Cross Crawl

This brain-eye exercise can easily be done standing, sitting, or supine with legs straight and arms down at the sides.

Breathe in and raise the right arm above the head while bending the left knee to raise leg.

Re-pattern by turning the head towards the raised arm. Then exhale and straighten the head as the arm and left leg come down.

Repeat with left arm & right leg, turning head towards the raised left arm.

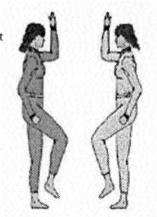

Do 12 right and 12 left for a total of 24 movements. Visualize marching.

May be done 50 to 100 times daily as a discipline practice.

Cross Crawl activates the brain for:
- Improved binocular (both eyes together) vision.
- Improved left/right coordination.
- Enhanced breathing and stamina.
- Greater coordination and spatial awareness.
- Enhanced hearing and vision.
- An ideal warm-up for all skills, especially academic skills and comprehension.

Figure Eight Energy Flows and Switching Points

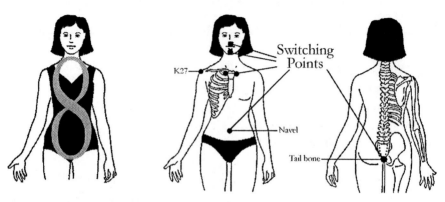

General Testing Review

Both subject and tester should remain relaxed and open to any result. The muscle test is a search for information. It is not a contest of strength.

Procedure

Stand erect with your best posture. Do not contract or recruit muscles other than the muscle being tested. Subject should look straight ahead, eyes open.

a. Place one hand on the subject's shoulder while lifting the arm into position. Then pause; wait about 6 seconds before pressing the arm down. Use a steady, light pressure (no more than the tester can exert with 2 fingers). Feel for the muscle lock using strength designed for the person being tested.

b. Do not overpower a muscle.

c. Make sure the subject understands the test before you proceed. Move the body through the range of motion gently but firmly, telling the subject to resist. Give the subject a moment to resist your pressure.

d. The first two inches of movement indicate the energy (the answer) regarding the question.

e. Keep the subject's hands from contacting their body and keep their legs uncrossed.

f. Breathe continuously. Do not hold your breath.

Muscle Testing for Yes or No Answers

Testing for Products

a. Put the substance on, or in front of the solar plexus.

b. Ask: Is this product for my highest good? Test.

c. If the muscle tests strong the answer is yes.

d. If the muscle tests weak the answer is no.

e. Repeat the procedure asking: Is this product harmful to me?

Testing for Lifestyle Questions

Refer to the Lifestyle Questions List

a. Ask: Is there a lifestyle change on this page that I should investigate? Test.

b. If the muscle tests strong the answer is yes.

c. If the muscle tests weak the answer is no.

Optional Testing Methods

Testing for Nutrition and Supplements

Start with a clear indicator muscle.

Ask: Do we have permission to test for this?

Go down the list, testing each item. A weak muscle indicates the item is not needed, a strong muscle indicates it is needed.

When looking at vitamins and other supplements use the Priority Testing Method. Hold thumb and index finger together.

Ask: We would now like to check for priority. Which supplement is the best? Go down the list, testing each item.

Surrogate Testing

Some cases may call for surrogate testing. Helper touches the person to be muscle tested and is tested in their place. The surrogate should be balanced before becoming a surrogate for another person. Have the person being tested touch the surrogate and perform the desired kinesiology procedure. This is a wonderful alternative for elderly, injured, sick and children.

To test for those who are not present, distance test using a surrogate, such as another person's arm, as follows.

Ask permission to use a surrogate. Make sure the person is clear about what they are doing and ready to be tested.

Ask the surrogate: Can I use your body to test for _____ at this time?

Ask the questions needed to clarify what supplements, nutrition or life questions need answering.

> *For sixty years I have been forgetful every moment,*
> *but not for one second has this flowing toward me*
> *stopped or slowed. I deserve nothing.*
> *Today I recognize that I am the guest the mystics*
> *talk about.*
> *I play this loving music for my Host.*
> *Everything I do is for the Host.*
>   ***Rumi***

Self Testing Methods

For self-testing instructions use these guidelines to test for any of the vibrational healing methods in this section. For testing others, see the Kinesiology Guidelines on pages 83-84.

Self Test – One

Hold thumb and index finger of one hand 2-3 inches apart depending on the size of your hand. With the other hand, place the thumb under the thumb of the first hand and two or three fingers of the second hand on the top of the index finger of the first hand. The testing is to attempt to bring the thumb and index finger together using slow even pressure.

Yes – Thumb and index stay apart

No – Thumb and index come together

Self Test – Two

Bring thumb and index finger together, forming a circle. Place the thumb and index finger of the opposite hand together and slip them into a circle created by the first hand. The movement is to spread the thumb and index finger of the second hand apart in the attempt to open the circle created by the position of the first hand. Apply slow even pressure.

Yes – Thumb and index come apart

No – Thumb and index stay together

Self Test – Three

Place the middle finger of your hand of choice on the index finger of the same hand. The action is to use the middle finger to attempt to push the index finger down.

Yes – Middle finger strong

No – Middle finger weak

Energy Evaluation Using a Pendulum

You may find that you prefer to use a pendulum for energy testing instead of muscle testing. One advantage of this method is that you can perform it without the use of your client's arm.

Guidelines for Pendulum Use

Accurate pendulum use requires that the practitioner stay alert and attentive while also being relaxed and tension free. Yoga breathing and prayer can help deepen intuition and a sense of selfless service. The pendulum is influenced by the attitudes held in the mind of the practitioner, so make every effort to maintain a detached frame of mind, remaining neutral and open to any answer.

     1. Hold the pendulum between the first finger and thumb and establish your yes or no answer. The pendulum will move on one of two axes, as shown in the drawing. Usually movement along the vertical axis (up and down) is yes and horizontal movement (back and forth) is no. It may also move in a clockwise circle for yes or counterclockwise for no. (See diagram)

     2. When working with the chakras and a pendulum place the pendulum over or in front of the chakra and observe the way it spins.

     3. If it doesn't spin, then the chakra could be inactive or under-energized. It may also spin in a counterclockwise manner, which indicates the energy is unbalanced. A clockwise manner should indicate the chakra is fully functioning. You can determine the differences between chakras and notice some are spinning more rapidly than others. These may require some balancing. Through breathing and affirmations you can often bring a particular chakra back into balance.

     4. You can also use the pendulum to discover the condition of a chakra by holding it over your palm chakra and asking about each of your chakras.

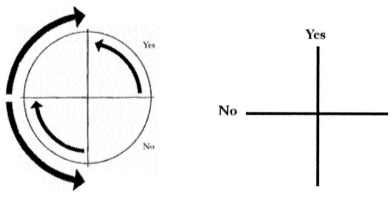

Clockwise and Counterclockwise　　　**Vertical Horizontal Axis**
Pendulum Swing　　　　　　　　　　　**Pendulum Swing**

Chapter Seven:

Kinesiology Testing Charts for Energy Well Being

In order to let go of something you must first know what it is.
Nisargadatta Maharaj, I Am That

Food Allergy and Nutritional Testing

To find out if a food or supplement is lacking or if there is too much, after a balance, hold the substance on the solar plexus chakra. Test. If it tests strong then that food is good for you, if weak, you could consider not using that particular food or substance for awhile.

Minerals

___ Calcium Fluoride	___ Calcium Phosphate	___ Calcium Sulphate
___ Iron Phosphate	___ Potassium Chloride	___ Potassium Phosphate
___ Potassium Sulphate	___ Magnesium Phosphate	___ Sodium Chloride
___ Nutrition	___ Allergy	___ Cell Salts
___ Minerals	___ Amino Acids	___ Enzymes

Food Supplements

___ Acidophilus	___ Alfalfa	___ Aloe Vera
___ Barley Grass	___ Bee Pollen	___ Betaine
___ Blue-Green Algae	___ Bromelain	___ Brewers Yeast
___ Chlorophyll	___ Cod Liver Oil	___ Coenzyme Q10
___ Liver Support	___ Fiber	___ GLA EFA
___ Lecithin	___ Garlic	___ Ginseng
___ Kelp	___ Omega 3 Flaxseed	___ Royal Jelly
___ Wheat Germ	___ Spirulina	

Foods

___ Berries	___ Beverages	___ Carbs
___ Chocolate	___ Fats and Oils	___ Flours
___ Fowl	___ Fruits	___ Grains
___ Herbs	___ Juice	___ Legume
___ Meat	___ Fish	___ Chicken
___ Beef	___ Lamb	___ Pork
___ Nuts	___ Seeds	___ Shellfish
___ Sprouts	___ Sugars	___ Vegetables
___ Water		

Systems

___ Spinal	___ Urinary	___ Circulatory	___ Psychological
___ Sympathetic	___ Respiratory	___ Digestive	___ Genital
___ Sensory	___ Chakra	___ Skeletal	___ Para-sympathetic
___ Musculature	___ Endocrine	___ Cells & Tissue	___ Lymphatic
___ Immune			

Amino Acids

___ Arginine	___ Aspartic Acid	___ Branch Chain
___ Cysteine	___ Carnitine	___ Glutamine
___ Di-Methyl Glycine	___ DLPA-DL Phenaladarine	___ Gaba
___ Ornithine	___ Gluthathione	___ Glycine
___ Hystine	___ Inosine	___ Lysine
___ Methionine	___ Phenalalarine	___ Taurine
___ Theonine	___ Tyrosine	

Essential and Trace Minerals

___ Boron	___ Calcium	___ Chlorine	___ Chromium
___ Cobalt	___ Copper	___ Flourine	___ Germanium
___ Gold	___ Iodine	___ Iron	___ Lithium
___ Magnesium	___ Manganese	___ Molyodenum	___ Phosphorous
___ Potassium	___ Selenium	___ Silicon	___ Sodium
___ Sulphur	___ Zinc		

Vitamins

___ A	___ Beta Carotene	___ B7 Biotin
___ B1 Thiamine	___ B2 Riboflavin	___ B3 Niacin
___ B8 Inositol	___ B5 Pantothenic Acid	___ B6 Pyridoxine
___ Bioflavonoids	___ B12 Cobalamin	___ B Complex
___ B9 Folic Acid	___ B4 Choline	___ B15 Pangamic Acid
___ C Ascorbic Acid	___ Calc. Pant.	___ D Viosterol
___ Ergosterol	___ E Tocopherol	___ K Menadione
___ Papa	___ Unsat. Fatty Acids	

Digestive Enzymes

___ Pancreatin	___ Papain

Endocrine System

___ Pineal	___ Pituitary	___ Mammary	___ Thyroid
___ Parotid	___ Thymus	___ Liver	___ Spleen
___ Lymph	___ Pancreas	___ Adrenal	___ Ovaries
___ Prostate	___ Testes		

Metals

___ Titanium	___ Hematite	___ Meteorite	___ Platinum
___ Copper	___ Silver	___ Gold	___ Pyrite
___ Zinc	___ Iron	___ Mercury	___ Arsenic
___ Aluminum	___ Lead		

Nutrition / Allergy Chart

Miscellaneous

Aspirin
Baking powder
Baking soda
Bancha green tea
Black tea
Carob
Chamomile
Chewing gum
Chocolate
Coffee
Coffee, Swiss, H$_2$o process,
　decaffeinated
Coffee, Sanka decaf
Gelatin
Kuzu
Licorice root
MSG
Nondairy creamer
Nutrisweet
Sweet & Low sweetener
Tapioca
Tobacco

Grains

Amaranth
Barley
Buckwheat
Cornmeal, blue
Cornmeal, white
Cornmeal, yellow
Cornstarch
Millet
Oat
Quinoa
Rice, brown

Rice, white
Rice, wild
Rye
Wheat
Wheat bran

Oils

Butter, cow milk (everclear)
Corn
Crisco
Margarine (everclear)
Olive
Safflower
Sesame
Soy

Milk & Cheese

Blue
Brie
Cheddar (raw milk)
Cottage
Hokkaido
Monterrey Jack
Muenster
Parmesan
Romano
Swiss
Cow milk, lowfat D
Goat milk
Sheep milk cheese
Lactose
Yogurt (cow milk)

Meat – Organic

Beef
Chicken
Lamb
Pork
Coconut

Meat – Nonorganic

Beef
Beef liver
Chicken
Lamb
Pork
Turkey

Seafood

Codfish – scrod
Haddock
Halibut
Mackerel
Octopus
Salmon
Crab
Swordfish
Tuna

Fruit – Non-organic

Apple, Rome
Apple, Yellow Delicious
Blueberry
Cantaloupe
Cherry, Bing
Current
Date
Grapes
Kiwi
Lemon
Lemon rind
Lime
Lime rind
Mango
Papaya
Pineapple
Raspberry
Strawberry
Tangerine
Watermelon

Fruit – Organic

Apple, Granny, Red Delicious
Banana
Grapefruit
Orange
Orange peel
Peach
Plum
Rhubarb

Spices

Allspice
Anise
Arrowroot
Basil
Bay leaf
Cayenne powder
Chicory root
Chili powder
Cinnamon
Cloves
Curry
Dill seed
Ginger
Horseradish Hops
Marjoram
Mustard
Nutmeg
Oregano
Paprika
Pepper, black
Sage
Salt, mineral (Spike)
Salt, miramoto
Salt, sea
Thyme
Vanilla bean

Nutrition / Allergy Chart – continued

Eggs
White
Yolk

Nuts
Almonds
Brazil
Cashew
Filbert
Peanut
Pecan
Pinenut
Walnut

Sea Vegetables
Agar agar
Arame
Dulse
Kelp
Kombu

Ferments – Liquor
Beer
Brandy
Gin
Vodka
Wine, red
Wine, white
Whiskey

Ferments – Liquid
Tamari
Tamari, wheatless
Vinegar, apple cider
Vinegar, balsamic
Vinegar, brown rice
Vinegar, umeboshi

Ferments – Solid
Miso, barley
Miso, brown rice
Yeast, baker's
Yeast, nutritional

Sweeteners
Barley
Beet sugar
Cane sugar
Fructose
Honey
Maple syrup
Rice bran syrup
Turbinado

Vegetables – Nonorganic
Artichoke
Asparagus
Bamboo shoots
Avocado
Broccoli
Brussels sprout
Cabbage
Carrots
Cauliflower
Celery
Chard
Collard green
Cucumber
Eggplant
Green beans
Potato
Radish

Snow peas
Squash, acorn
Squash, winter
Squash, summer
Turnip
Watercress
Leek
Lettuce – romaine,
    iceberg
Lotus root
Mushroom
Okra

Vegetables – Organic
Beets
Broccoli
Carrots
Cabbage, green
Cucumber
Daikon root
Kale
Lettuce – leaf,
    romaine, butter
Potato, white
Pumpkin
Spinach
Squash, delicate
Squash, zucchini
Swiss Chard
Tomato

Tissue Salts

Wilhelm Heinrich Schuessler originated the twelve tissue salts, also called cell salts. He found that there are certain important inorganic substances that need to be present in order for cells to work effectively and that the deficiency of these substances is often responsible for physical disorders. Tissue salts are the principal inorganic substances found in the cells of the human body and are essential to cellular metabolism. They allow the cells to be properly nourished, to cleanse and regenerate themselves. The salts are prepared and administered in homeopathic potencies of about 6X, which makes them readily assimilated by the body.

The practitioner is helped by knowing how the tissue salts work individually. He then has a lead on applying them to the symptoms of any given case. Use of the pendulum can confirm the choice of salts for treatment. In cases where two remedies are equally indicated, they should be taken alternately. In acute cases, the doses may be taken every half hour; in less acute cases, every two hours is recommended and in chronic cases, three or four times daily.

Calcium Fluoride (Calc. Fluor.)

This tissue salt gives elasticity to the tissues. It is bound in the walls of blood vessels, connective tissue, and in muscular tissue. When it is absent, tissue develops a relaxed condition. Calcium Fluoride preserves the contractile power of elastic tissue. Symptoms of relaxed tissue include piles, sluggish circulation and fissures in the palms of the hands and between the toes. This salt is used to treat diseases, which attack the surface of the bones and joints, and loose and decaying teeth. Muscular weakness is also treated with Calcium Fluoride.

Calcium Phosphate (Calc. Phos.)

This tissue salt assists the coagulator for blood. It helps to form hair and teeth and restores tone to weakened organs and tissues. It is concerned with nutrition, and is important to growing children, where it is specific for rickets. It helps speed recuperation, improves blood where anemic conditions prevail, assists digestion and, coincidentally, promotes good circulation.

Calcium Sulphate (Calc. Sulph.)

This tissue salt is a blood purifier. It promotes the removal of waste material in the liver and has a general cleansing influence in the whole system, helping tissues to throw off toxic substances. It is often recommended for acne, purifying the blood and clearing up abscesses before they become septic. It can offset the early stages of a sore throat or infection.

Tissue Salts – continued

Iron Phosphate (Ferr. Phos.)

This substance helps the blood to carry oxygen, by building up the red blood cells. It is often used as a supplementary remedy with other cell salts. Symptoms of oxygen deficiency include quickened pulse, congestion, inflammatory pain and high temperature. It is used where there are hemorrhages, and in cases of anemia.

Potassium Chloride (Kali. Mur.)

This salt is the cure for sluggish conditions, symptomized by thick white discharges, creating catarrhs that affect the skin and mucous membrane. Both potassium chloride and calcium sulphate are concerned with purifying the blood. In cases requiring potassium chloride, the blood tends to thicken and clot. Symptoms include: white-coated tongue, light colored stools, slow liver action, frequent coughs and colds and bronchitis.

Potassium Phosphate (Kali. Phos.)

This is a nerve nutrient, good for nervous disorders. It may be useful in cases of fretfulness, ill humor, bashfulness, laziness and timidity, or what are called "tantrums" among children. Other conditions, which may be alleviated by this substance, are nervous headaches, nervous indigestion, sleeplessness, tiredness and low vitality, depression, irritability, and general listlessness.

Potassium Sulphate (Kali. Sulph.)

This salt helps in the oxygen exchange from blood to cell tissues, and is helpful in respiratory problems. Wherever there are sticky, yellowish discharges from the skin or mucous membrane, this tissue salt is recommended. Skin eruptions are helped by potassium sulphate, as are intestinal disorders and stomach cramps.

Whatever I do, the responsibility is mine but like one who plants an orchard, what comes of what I do, the fruit will be for this. I offer the actions of this life to God within and wherever I go, the way is blessed.

Lalla – Naked Song
by Coleman Barks

Magnesium Phosphate (Mag. Phos.)

This is the antispasmodic tissue salt, and supplements the action of potassium phosphate. Deficiency of this tissue salt causes the white nerve fibers to contract, producing spasms and cramps. This salt is a fast pain reliever in such cases, and also in cases of neuralgia, neuritis, sciatica, and stabbing headaches. It helps in cases of muscular twitching, hiccups, convulsive coughing, and cramps, especially such of the foregoing as are accompanied by sharp spasmodic pains.

Sodium Chloride (Nat. Mur.)

This is the water distributing salt, part of every fluid and solid in the body, where it maintains proper moisture distribution. It is related to nutrition, glandular activity and internal secretions. Excessive dryness or moisture is a symptom indicating the need for this tissue salt. Some of the following symptoms are also indicators: low spirits with a feeling of hopelessness; headaches with constipation; thin blood; pallor of the skin, which sometimes has a greasy appearance; difficult stools, with rawness and soreness of the anus; colds with discharge of watery mucus and sneezing; dry, painful nose and throat; heartburn due to gastric fermentation with slow digestion; great thirst; toothache and facial neuralgia with flow of tears and saliva; weak, sensitive eyes; hay fever; drowsiness with muscular weakness; chafing of the skin; hangnails; unrefreshing sleep; after-effects of alcoholic stimulants; loss of taste and smell; craving for salt and salty foods.

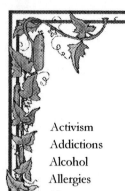

Lifestyle Questions
Possible life issues for kinesiology testing
Test Yes or No if any of the below need attention.

Activism	Hobbies	Reading Material
Addictions	Home	Relationship to higher power
Alcohol	Integrity	Relationships
Allergies	Internet	Relaxation
Alone	Life Shocks	Rest
Attitude	Life-style Testing	Rhythm
Automobile	Life-style Testing Charts	Romance
Behavior	Love	Sabbatical
Caffeine	Manipulation	Sacred Space
Career	Mealtimes	School
Cell Salts	Medication	Services
Change of Job	Medicine	Simplicity
Change of Locality	Meditation	Sleep
Change of Partner	Minerals	Soul Mate
Change of Residence	Money	Soul Rest
Chaos	Moving	Soul Searching
Children's Issues	Music	Spiritual Growth
Choice of Products	Nature	Spiritual Practice
Co-dependence	Need for Clear Intention	Sports
Computer	Need for Meditation	Sunlight
Creative Outlets	Need for Prayer	Supplements
Daily Emotions	Need for Quiet	Support
Daily thoughts	Need Referral	Teacher
Devotion	Need to be alone	Television
Diet	Need Vibrational Support	Therapist Choice
Drugs	News	Trips
Energy Drain	Nonscheduled time	Vacation
Energy Field Wellness	Nutrition	Vitamins
Environmental Toxins	Order	Walking
Exercise	Organization	
Family Ties	Outdoor	
Fitness	Over-caring Issues	
Follow Joy	Parents' Issues	
Garden	Personal Products	
Geopathic Stress	Products	
Guru	Radio	
Health Questions		

Chapter Eight:

Vibrational Medicine –
An Energy Healer's Toolbox

Love is the meaning and purpose of duality.
Nisargadatta Maharaj, I Am That

The Bach Flowers and Flower Essences

Dr. Edward Bach first developed the Bach Flowers in 1930 as treatments for the causes of illness in the emotional and mental energy fields. Dr. Bach believed that illness could not be treated effectively without taking emotional, mental and spiritual influences into consideration. His work with flower essences was based on the premise that the heart and soul held the answers to tuning negative emotional and health states to positive states.

Dr. Bach defined thirty-eight different emotional states, along with seven states of mind. Bach discovered that correcting beliefs, attitudes and conditioning can stop the onset of disease. The mental components that lay at the root of the problems can be corrected through flower remedies, which illuminate negative aspects of the personality and encourage the positive expression of energy.

The remedies balance disturbances in the emotional, mental and spiritual bodies to prevent physical illness. Dr. Bach realized that illness was a symptom of disharmony between soul and personality. He believed all beings had a divine purpose and illness was a message for one to see their error in perception and find their true purpose.

Some of the core soul issues that Bach felt were the cause of illness are impatience, a critical attitude, grief, excessive fear, terror, bitterness, lack of self esteem, over-enthusiasm, indecision, doubt, ignorance, denial or repression, resentment, restlessness, apathy, indifference, weakness of will and guilt.

The positive soul virtues of love, wisdom, courage, joy, strength, vigilance, harmlessness, forgiveness, understanding, acceptance, compassion are encouraged through the flowers. They reconnect the personality with soul and create an energy alignment between the lower fields and the spiritual fields.

Flower essences are made from many types of flowers from around the world. Blossoms are picked in their prime and floated in vats of pure distilled water, which are exposed to sunlight. The subtle essence of the flowers is transferred by means of the light into the water. Brandy, vinegar or glycerine is added as a preservative.

In choosing a remedy, let the state of mind guide the choice of which remedies are necessary. Observe the state of mind for any change in the thought process. It is important to note these changes before disease appears so that treatment can prevent the onset of disease. When an illness has been present for a long time the mood of the sufferer will guide to the correct remedy.

Guidelines for Using Flower Essences

2–4 drops under tongue, four times a day or every hour.

Doses can be taken in water, milk, juice or any convenient manner.

May be taken every few minutes. For severe symptoms, every half-hour. For long-standing conditions take every 2–3 hours.

Up to seven Flower Essences can be mixed in a dropper bottle and administered as above either under the tongue or in a small amount of water.

Bach Flower Rescue Remedy

Rescue Remedy is a combination of Clematis, Cherry Plum, Impatiens, Rock Rose, Star of Bethlehem and is effective for sudden shock, emotional upheaval, stress, loss, grief or any disturbance. This mixture can assist in relieving urgent symptoms within 20 minutes. Rescue Remedy can be taken for all stressful situations, for people, animals or plants. Up to five drops either under the tongue or in water.

How to use Bach Flowers – Kinesiology Testing

Soul Dialogue is an exploration that reveals which Bach Flowers will be beneficial to your healing and transformation path. This inquiry can identify soul issues related to the present, future or past and identify remedies to assist in releasing blocks that prevent you from living your full potential.

To perform the test, hold the selected remedy in one hand, preferably near the solar plexus of yourself or person being tested. With the other hand test a muscle. If the muscle tests strong then the remedy will be supportive of the healing path.

Preparation of Flower Remedies

First choose the flowers you wish to prepare essence from and then pick them fresh. Place them in a clear glass bowl filled with spring water. Place the bowl of flowers and water in the early morning sunlight. The essence of the flower will infuse the water with healing vibrations. Put a preservative in the essence such as brandy or vinegar or glycerin. After preparing the remedy, pound it against your palm 100 times, this infuses the healing energies into the water.

In a glass dropper take one ounce of water to four drops of concentrated flower essence. Take four drops, four times daily, under the tongue, or in juice, water or milk.

Essences assist with recurrent issues and deep-seated emotional and mental patterns. The flower essences also assist in deep transformation and consciousness change and support your healing intention. Through releasing negative recurring thoughts they change self-destructive tendencies and break the habits of worry, fear and anxiety. Flower essences also release toxic emotions such as resentment, grief, guilt, hatred, victim-hood. They also release mental conclusions and limiting belief systems in the mind, opening doors to new possibilities of freedom and well being.

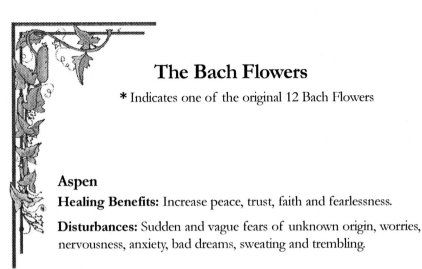

The Bach Flowers

* Indicates one of the original 12 Bach Flowers

Aspen

Healing Benefits: Increase peace, trust, faith and fearlessness.

Disturbances: Sudden and vague fears of unknown origin, worries, nervousness, anxiety, bad dreams, sweating and trembling.

Agrimony *

Healing Benefits: Increase joy and cheerfulness.

Disturbances: Repression and denial of feelings of pain and discomfort. For those who seek excitement, loneliness, who are distressed by arguments, avoid conflict, are worried and restless.

Beech

Healing Benefits: Increase tolerance and understanding, strong convictions, high ideals.

Disturbances: Intolerance of others, overly critical, lacking in humility, strong convictions, finding fault with others, judgmental, arrogant and extremely prejudiced.

Centaury *

Healing Benefits: Self-determination, wisdom and a strong sense of self.

Disturbances: For the weak willed and those who can't stand up for themselves, who behave like a doormat and cannot say no. For those who constantly try to please others, who fear telling the truth, do not like to make waves or displease others. Effective for issues of co-dependency and feelings of victimhood.

Cerato *

Healing Benefits: Inner trust, wisdom and commitment.

Disturbances: Self-doubt, foolishness, needing advice all the time, lack of self-trust and confidence in own judgment.

The Bach Flowers – continued

Cherry Plum

Healing Benefits: Courage, balance under any situation and calmness.

Disturbances: Suicidal thoughts, fear of insanity, violent impulses, nervous breakdown, desperate situations, constant frictions, deep despair.

Chestnut Bud

Healing Benefits: Observant, learning life's lessons, gaining knowledge and wisdom from life's experience.

Disturbances: Failure to learn, lack of observation, repeating mistakes and lack of humility.

Chicory *

Healing Benefits: Selfless care and concern for others, always giving without thought of return.

Disturbances: Possessiveness and selfishness, easily hurt, offended, feelings of rejection, need constant attention and dislike being alone.

Clematis *

Healing Benefits: Inspirational, hopeful, idealistic, down to earth, realistic, and take a lively interest in life.

Disturbances: Indifference, fainting, drowsiness, daydreaming, unhappiness, coma condition and prefering to be alone.

Crab Apple

Healing Benefits: Cleansing for mind and body, helps to put things in perspective, good for self control, increases harmony and balance.

Disturbances: Feelings of despair, uncleanness, disgust or shame.

Elm

Healing Benefits: Increases efficiency, intuition, the ability to follow an inner call, a feeling of service, faith and confidence.

Disturbances: Being overwhelmed, too much responsibility, exhaustion, depression, weakness and debility.

Gentian *

Healing Benefits: Conquering all obstacles, lack of failure, not affected by setbacks, and great conviction of purpose.

Disturbances: Discouragement, despondency, depression, lack of faith, negative outlook, long term or recurring illness and long convalescence.

Gorse

Healing Benefits: Positive faith and hope, feelings of great strength, uninfluenced by opinions of others.

Disturbances: Hopelessness, despair and a feeling that pain is too much.

Heather

Healing Benefits: Selflessness, understanding and a willingness to help others.

Disturbances: Self-centeredness, self-concern, obsessed by personal problems, sometimes weepy, saps the vitality of others, dislikes being alone and a poor listener.

Holly

Healing Benefits: Vibration of Divine Love. Imparts generosity, rejoicing, understanding and tolerance.

Disturbances: Negative thoughts and emotions such as jealously, envy, revenge and suspicion. Sometimes feels aggressive and greedy. For those who suffer inner unhappiness and an absence of love.

Honeysuckle

Healing Benefits: Letting go of past, present-centeredness, helps put memories in perspective and extract essential value from them.

Disturbances: Living in the past, homesickness, regrets, fear of the future and a loss of interest in the present.

The Bach Flowers – continued

Hornbeam

Healing Benefits: Clearing and increasing mental vitality and increasing strength to deal with life.

Disturbances: Weariness and mental fatigue, doubts own strength, finds life burdensome, self-preoccupied and tired.

Impatiens *

Healing Benefits: Relaxation, patience, tolerance and gentleness.

Disturbances: Assertive, irritable, impatient, nervous, accident prone, feels mental tension through frustrations and other pressures.

Larch

Healing Benefits: Release of fears, capable, not discouraged, willing to take risks and live with an "I can" attitude.

Disturbances: Lack of confidence, convinced of failure, feelings of being not good enough or capable, chronic low self-esteem and feelings of inferiority.

Mimulus *

Healing Benefits: Brings courage, equanimity, humor and lightness. Increases understanding and faith.

Disturbances: Fear of known things, stage fright, stammering, nervousness, secret fears, shyness and timidity.

Mustard

Healing Benefits: Inner serenity, peace, joy and cheerfulness.

Disturbances: Deep depression, intense gloom, melancholia, hopelessness and an overwhelming sense of doom.

Oak

Healing Benefits: Courage, stability, reliable, inner strength, common sense, patience and bravery.

Disturbances: Despondency, hopelessness, grave difficulties, illness and disconnected with self.

Olive

Healing Benefits: Revitalization, renewed interest in life, quietness, peace and clarity of mind.

Disturbances: Complete exhaustion, difficult convalescence, long illness, mental fatigue and a loss of vital force.

Pine

Healing Benefits: Responsible, great perseverance, humility and sound judgment.

Disturbances: Self-reproach, guilt, blame of oneself, self-critical, takes on blame of others, hard working, and perfectionist.

Red Chestnut

Healing Benefits: Positive thoughts of safety and care for others, encouragement and the ability to remain calm in an emergency.

Disturbances: Anxiety for others, negative thoughts, fearful, fretful and worried.

Rock Rose *

Healing Benefits: Great courage, willing to take risks for others and great inner strength.

Disturbances: Terror, fear, extreme shock, panic, trauma, acute threats, natural disaster and sudden illness.

Rock Water

Healing Benefits: Flexibility, not easily influenced by others, peace and joy, relief from strictness and the ability to adapt.

Disturbances: Depression and denial, over concentration on self, hard taskmaster, self-denial, martyrdom and uptightness.

The Bach Flowers – continued

Scleranthus *

Healing Benefits: Good for children, calmness, determination, poise and balance.

Disturbances: Uncertainty, unreliable, indecision, hesitancy, swayed between two opposites such as joy and sadness, energy and apathy, optimism and pessimism, laughing and crying.

Sweet Chestnut

Healing Benefits: Full control of emotions, strong character, faith and miracles

Disturbances: Great anguish, mental despair, at the limit of endurance, exhaustion, depression and finding life too difficult.

Star of Bethlehem

Healing Benefits: Releases trauma, brings peace and faith

Disturbances: Grief, sudden shocks, fright of an accident and loss of a loved one. A remedy for crisis of any kind.

Vervain *

Healing Benefits: Great courage, shows by example, faces danger, calm, wise and tolerant.

Disturbances: Tenseness, anxiety, stress, high strung, fanatical and argumentative.

Vine

Healing Benefits: Capable, confident, assured, balanced and flexible and helps others in self-knowledge.

Disturbances: Domineering, inflexible, opinionated, demanding, expects obedience, aggressive pride, greedy for authority, knows better than anyone, arrogant and needs power.

Walnut

Healing Benefits: Idealistic, protection from effects of change, helpful for transitions and life changes, relieves stressful situations.

Disturbances: Oversensitive, affected by others, influenced by others.

Water Violet *

Healing Benefits: Quiet, gentle, tranquil, wise, independent, self-reliant and capable. Brings peace, calm and blessings to those around. Needs solitude.

Disturbances: Proud, aloof, disdainful, condescending, mentally rigid and tense.

White Chestnut

Healing Benefits: Peace and quiet, self-controlled and clarity of mind.

Disturbances: Argumentative, worried, troubled by distressing thoughts, sleepless and lacking concentration.

Wild Oat

Healing Benefits: Lives life feeling useful and with great happiness, clarity in life, direction and vocation.

Disturbances: Uncertainty regarding path in life, undecided, unclear, despondent, dissatisfied, frustrated, depressed and tries many things but none brings happiness.

Wild Rose

Healing Benefits: Lively interest in life, ambitious and purposeful.

Disturbances: Resigned, apathetic, resigned to illness, surrendered, hopeless, weary, and lacking in vitality.

Willow

Healing Benefits: Optimism and faith, takes responsibility, neutral and releases bitterness from the past.

Disturbances: Resentment, bitterness, self-pity, blames others, begrudges life, irritable, not interested in affairs of others, ungrateul and alienating.

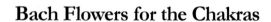

Bach Flowers for the Chakras

Root Chakra

Cherry Plum: Letting go

Clematis: Grounding

Gorse: Integration

Pine: Taking responsibility

Sweet Chestnut: Trusting yourself

Navel Chakra

Crab apple: Getting rid of what you can't digest

Elm: Turning your ideas into reality

Mimulus: Enjoying freedom within a fixed structure

Oak: Surrender

Rock Water: Discipline with release

Vervain: Accepting others

Wild Rose: Taking part in life joyfully and fully

Solar Plexus Chakra

Aspen: Overcoming fear

Hornbeam: Being able to achieve personal goals

Impatiens: Patience

Larch: Self-awareness

Scleranthus: Balance within yourself

Star of Bethlehem: Ability to act from inner joy

The Healing of Chakras through Bach Flowers

Heart Chakra
Centaury: Service

Chicory: Overcoming distance

Heather: Unconditional love

Holly: Free-flowing love energy

Honeysuckle: Living in the here and now

Red Chestnut: The ability to express true love

Rock rose: Overcoming ego limitations

Throat Chakra
Agrimony: Fusing thinking and feeling

Mustard: Trusting yourself even in difficult times

Wild oat: Communicating from your deepest soul

Willow: Making space for creativity

Third Eye Chakra
Beech: Tolerance

Cerato: Following your inner guide

Chestnut Bud: Being open to learning from life

Gentian: Acceptance

Olive: Trusting, cosmic harmony

Vine: Accepting authority

Walnut: Being able to listen to you inner voice

White Chestnut: An aid to mediation

Flower Essences

(See guidelines on how to use flower essences, pp. 103-104.)
These may be purchased through Flower Essence Society; see
the reference section of the book.

Agrimony: Assists in getting in touch with deep soul disturbances and
helps to increase emotional honesty.

Aloe Vera: Creative activity becomes balanced and centered in vital life
energy. Increases harmony and mental rejuvenation. Relieves impatience.

Alpine Valley: For women, acceptance of one's femininity, grounded in
a deepened experience of the female body.

Angel's Trumpet: Spiritual surrender at death or at time of deep
transformation, opening the heart to the spiritual world.

Angelica: Increases angelic connections and spiritual rejuvenation. Brings divine
protection and guidance. Awakens perceptions, assists one to have courage and
inner strength.

Arnica: Conscious embodiment, especially during shock or recovery from deep-
seated trauma.

Aspen: Brings a sense of inner trust, confidence, strength and protection from
astral influences.

Baby Blue Eyes: Childlike innocence and trust, feeling at home in this world, at
ease with oneself, supported and loved; connected with the spiritual world.

Basil: Integration of sexuality into a sacred wholeness.

Black Cohosh: Courage to confront rather than retreat from abusive or threaten-
ing situations.

Blackberry: For manifesting creative inspiration and for opening to new levels
of consciousness.

Black-eyed Susan: Awakens consciousness making it capable of acknowledging
all aspects of the personality. Helps release resistance to looking at emotions.

Bleeding Heart: Loving others unconditionally, with an open heart, emotional
freedom. Good heart healer. Helps heal broken relationships and brings peace,
harmony and balance to the heart.

Borage: Heart remedy, especially for the feeling of heaviness in the heart.
Excellent all-purpose formula.

Buttercup: Helps soul realize and sustain inner light. For those who feel inadequate.

Calla Lily: Clarity about sexual identity.

Calendula: Awakens the healing power of words.

California Poppy: Increases intuition, helps one to see the aura.

California Wild Rose: Promotes love for earth and human life and enthusiasm for doing and serving.

Chaparral: Brings about psychic awareness. Detoxifies the system.

Canyon Dudleya: Balances psychic and physical energies.

Cayenne: Ignites and sparks the soul to assist in initiating and sustaining emotional development.

Chamomile: Promotes emotional balance. Helps release tension from stomach and solar plexus areas. Subdues small emotions.

Chrysanthemum: Shifts ego identification from one's personality to higher spiritual identity.

Corn: Alignment with earth, especially through body and feet; grounded presence.

Columbine: Increases self-appreciation, self-love and personal power.

Comfrey: Repairs soul damage.

Cosmos: Promotes integration of ideas and speech; ability to express thoughts with coherence and clarity.

Deerbrush: Promotes gentle purity, clarity of purpose and sincerity of motive.

Dandelion: For dynamic and effortless energy; lively activity balanced with inner ease.

Dill: Aids in experiencing and absorbing the fullness of life.

Dogwood: Allows grace-filled movement, physical and etheric harmony. Clarifies emotions and turning to spiritual sources.

Easter Lily: Promotes inner purity of soul, especially the ability to integrate sexuality and spirituality.

Echinacea: A fundamental remedy for many soul and physical illnesses.

Evening Primrose: Helps to open the heart.

Flower Essences – continued

Fairy Lantern: Releases emotional blocks that occurred in childhood.

Fawn Lily: Promotes integration of spirituality in the world.

Filaree: Assists one to put life in perspective and promotes cosmic understanding.

Five Flower Formula: Promotes calmness and stability in an emergency. Consists of cherry plum, clematis, impatiens, rock rose, star of Bethlehem.

Forget-me-not: For awareness of karmic connections.

Fuchsia: Promotes emotional vitality and the ability to express feelings.

Garlic: Heals fragmented souls.

Gentian: Good for life setbacks, discouragement, disheartenment, need for solutions. Increases trust.

Golden Ear Drops: Helps one to remember emotional disturbances from the past.

Golden Yarrow: Promotes opened, balanced, inner protection, integrity of health and well being.

Golden Rod: Promotes well developed individuality or personal power.

Gorse: For deep abiding faith.

Heather: Promotes inner tranquility, emotional self-esteem.

Hibiscus: Brings soul dignity for women, helps heal sexual trauma.

Holly: Aids in feeling love and extending love to others.

Honeysuckle: Helps to be fully in the present, learning lessons from the past.

Hornbeam: Promotes energy, enthusiasm, involved with life's work.

Hound's Tongue: Aids in thinking in terms of wholeness, integration of spirit and world.

Impatiens: Promotes patience, acceptance, flowing with the pace of life.

Indian Paintbrush: Makes one lively, energetic and able to express spirituality.

Indian Pink: Helps to remain centered and focused under stress.

Iris: Inspires artistry, building bridge of light between spirit and matter. Symbolizes hope and eternal spirit.

Lady's Slipper: Integrates spiritual purpose and daily work.

Larch: Promotes self-confidence, creative expression, spontaneity.

Larkspur: Brings charismatic leadership.

Lotus: Aids inspirational, healing, opens intuition, reconnects with one's divine source, affects crown chakra.

Lavender: Soothes nerves and over-sensitivity to psychic and spiritual experiences.

Madia: Focuses concentration, clear thinking.

Mallow: Opens heart, sharing, friendliness.

Manzanita: Integrates spiritual self with world.

Mariposa Lily: Helps to show nurturing and caring attention for others.

Milkweed: Promotes healthy ego, strength, independence, self-reliance.

Morning Glory: Brings sparkling vital force, in touch with life.

Mimulus: Aids courage and confidence to face life's challenges.

Mountain Pennyroyal: Promotes strength and clarity of thought.

Mountain Pride: Helps to take a stand in the world and be a spiritual warrior.

Mugwort: Awakens greater awareness of spiritual influence, brings in more consciousness.

Mullein: Strengthens sense of inner consciousness, truthfulness and uprightness. Being true to oneself.

Mustard: Promotes emotional equanimity, finding joy in life.

Nasturtium: Brings glowing vitality, radiant energy.

Nicotiana: Brings emotional well being, peace, inner strength and stability.

Oak: Balances strength, accepting life and knowing when to surrender.

Olive: Revitalizes through connection with one's inner source of energy.

Oregon Grape: Promotes trust in the goodness of others, loving kindness.

Flower Essences – continued

Peony: Assists the heart center to open and increases deep love of self and unconditional love for others. Opens one to the presence of God within.

Penstemon: Brings great inner strength despite outer hardships.

Peppermint: Promotes mindfulness, waking clarity.

Pine: Helps to release guilt, blaming self for the mistakes of others.

Pink Monkey Flower: Provides emotional openness and honesty.

Pink Yarrow: Promotes compassion and openness to the feelings of others.

Poison Oak: Promotes emotional vulnerability.

Pomegranate: Brings sense of warmhearted feminine creativity.

Pretty Face: Promotes beauty that radiates from within.

Purple Monkey Flower: Provides sense of inner calm, trust in spiritual guidance, release from fear.

Pine: Promotes self-acceptance, self-forgiveness, freedom from guilt and shame.

Quaking Grass: Brings harmonious soul consciousness, balanced life.

Queen Anne's Lace: Strengthens spiritual insight and visualization, integration of mind and emotions.

Quince: Balances masculine and feminine powers.

Rabbitbrush: Maintains flexible state of mind.

Red Clover: Cleanses, balances, maintains strong self-awareness.

Red Chestnut: Promotes caring for others with inner peace, calmness and trust in the unfolding of life's events.

Rock Rose: Enhances self-transcendence, courage, inner peace, tranquility when facing great challenges.

Rock Water: Brings flexibility, flowing reception, following spiritual guidance.

Rose: Awakens love and inspiration, helps attune to the angelic hierarchies.

Rosemary: Stimulates mental facilities. Aid to purify body, mind and emotions.

Rhubarb: Good for boundary issues, insecurity and vulnerability.

Sage: Increases understanding of true self, stimulates the mind.

Sagebrush: Deepens awareness of inner self, letting go of false images.

Saguaro: Brings awareness of ancient memories, assists ability to learn, clarity in relationship to authority and guidance.

Saint John's Wart: Opens one to divine guidance. Releases hidden fear from past lives. Good for depression.

Scarlet Monkey Flower: Good for emotional honesty.

Scotch Broom: Promotes positive and optimistic feelings in the world, caring, encouragement and perception.

Self-Heal: Excellent for soul healing and balance, enhances self-healing powers, self-confidence and self-acceptance.

Shasta Daisy: Integrates thinking part with analytical aspect of mind.

Shooting Star: Helps one to find right connection with earthly life, helps with feeling at home on earth.

Snapdragon: Helps soul for greater creative focus.

Star Thistle: Releases fear of "lack." Promotes inner sense of abundance.

Star Tulip: The "listening remedy." Opening one to guidance from higher realm.

Star of Bethlehem: Brings soothing, healing qualities and a sense of inner divinity.

Stinging Nettle: Eases all emotional stress. Nettle helps as a tonic for the kidneys, lungs and nervous system.

Sunflower: Promotes expression of individuality. Balances ego, helps with self-esteem.

Sweet Chestnut: Deep courage and faith, knowing and trusting the spiritual world.

Sticky Mountain Flower: Heals challenges with intimacy.

Sun Flower: Brings light to the soul.

Sweet Pea: Helps soul come into contact with feelings of shame.

Tansy: Helps with being decisive, aide's lethargy, procrastination and decision making.

Tiger Lily: Increases feminine forces. Helps with meno-pause.

Flower Essences – continued

Trillium: Increases energy for selfless service.

Trumpet Vine: Good to assist in verbal expression.

Vervain: Increases ability to practice moderation, tolerance and balance.

Vine: Promotes selfless service, tolerance, strong will and leadership.

Violet: Awakens one to the spiritual side of manifestation.

Walnut: Helps free one from limiting influences, transitions in life, courage to follow one's own path.

Water Violet: Enables sharing one's gifts with others, quiet and self-contained.

White Chestnut: Promotes inner quiet, calm and clear mind.

Wild Oat: Works as an expression of inner calling; in outward life, one experiences one's true goal and values.

Willow: Promotes acceptance, forgiveness, taking responsibility, flowing with life.

Wild Rose: Aids those who have given up hope.

Yellow Star Tulip: Brings empathy, receptivity to feelings experienced of others.

Yerba Santa: The "Holy Herb" harmonizes breath with feeling.

Yarrow: Assists in conditions such as environmental illness, allergies, psychosomatic diseases, psychic shielding, boundaries, and protection.

Yarrow Special Formula: General tonic and strengthener to help meet harsh technological and environmental challenges in the modern world. Use before and after exposure to radiation. When subjected to forces of geopathic stress, strong electromagnetic fields and other forms of environmental toxicity. To strengthen the immune system. During times of extreme stress, with core issues of integrity and identity. For those with pronounced sensitivity, during traveling, in large crowds. Action of this formula is on an etheric level.

Zinnia: Promotes childlikeness and playfulness, joyful in the light, profound sense of self.

Essential Oils and Healing Fragrances

Ancient Egyptians have used essential oils daily since 1500 BC. Essential oils such as frankincense, sandalwood, myrrh, rosemary and hyssop have been used for anointing and healing the sick for centuries. Essential oils, like flower essences, change the frequency of negative patterns that are locked into the energy fields.

Changing belief systems, becoming conscious of held patterns, seeing a new direction and releasing and reprogramming the subconscious, letting go of limitations and labels are assisted through the use of essential oils as well as flower remedies.

Emotions and belief systems are basically frozen energy that needs to be resolved and released. Giving the energy system a different message, such as the positive side of the emotion, brings more vitality into the energy field and provides a goal or healing path to travel through. When the mental field is connected with the higher spiritual energy fields, it has a strong impact on the emotional field. The higher impressions of truth, honesty, aspiration, trust and clarity are more powerful than the negative self-limiting emotions and beliefs. Through working with a soul's goal or healing intention, the self-limiting energy will be released.

Through kinesiology, patterns are identified in the energy fields that cause disturbance and energy drains. Usually the pattern is connected to a desire pattern that has implanted in the emotional field or a belief system about something one wants. When these discordant energy patterns are understood one can work with the soul's truth to find a wiser way to be in life. Through understanding life's problems in the light of the soul, there is a greater thrust in removing obstacles to being in the light. The light brings a great joy and peace to one's life. Once negative patterns are identified, one discovers a goal healing intention to assist in their release.

The vibrational remedy that supports this energy release is chosen through kinesiology testing. When the discordant energy pattern is identified, the way out, or healing intention, becomes the soul affirmation. Through sacred dialogue the healing intention draws the negative energy out of its frozen or stuck state. Put goals and affirmations in the present time, using "I" statements such as "I am ____," or "I will ____," affirming and being in the present time with the new reality. Creating a new reality means envisioning how you want it to be and believing you can transform your reality to this new vision.

Essential Oils – Nature's Fragrant Garden

Aromas are pure fragrances for healing body, mind and spirit. You can use the aromas in the form of incense, flower essences, and essential oils, or soaps, candles, and sachets. Aromatherapy is used externally and most aromas are diluted with a base oil or carrier oil. Some of the carrier oils that can be chosen are sesame, coconut, sunflower, canola, mustard, sweet almond, avocado, calendula, carrot, hazelnut, jojoba, olive, peanut and wheat germ.

Steps to Release Emotional Stress

Use kinesiology to identify the emotion (see the emotional healing section.) Create an affirmation, or soul's goal, that increases the positive emotion that you want to receive from the balance. Ask for a gift of the spirit or soul lesson. Use the emotional stress release technique and apply oils at the emotional points on the forehead, chakras, alarm points, hands or feet. They can also be applied to the points specified in the etheric revitalization treatment.

1. Identify and feel the emotions.
2. Smell the oil.
3. Identify the positive emotion or healing intention.
4. Apply oil to specific area.
5. Create a new life-affirming affirmation.
6. Apply oils to the Ayurvedic acupressure points.

 Rise up nimbly and go on your strange journey to the ocean of meanings. The stream knows it can't stay on the mountain. Leave and don't look away, from the sun as you go, in whose light your sometimes crescent, sometimes full.
Rumi

Ayurvedic Acupressure Points for application of essential oils

- Third Eye (between eyebrows)

- Heart Chakra (chest center)

- Between the navel and pubic bone.

Emotional Stress Release Points

On the forehead, divide the forehead in two. The emotional stress release points are halfway between the eyebrow and the hairline in the hollow of the forehead.

Using kinesiology, identify the emotion and the chakra that the emotion is related to, or the belief pattern. Create a healing intention or soul affirmation and then apply the oil to the emotional points, the frontal eminences. Hold the points while stating the affirmation, and visualize the story that the emotion or belief is attached to as if on a movie screen. Wait for the pulses to synchronize and then retest. If the arm is strong, it indicates the emotion or limiting belief has been diffused or released. Oils can be applied to chakras, alarm points, and emotional stress points and the point at the base of the neck called the release point. Oils can also be applied to points on the feet, such as K1, and to many points on the hand. Apply to the hand and rotate clockwise to activate.

How to Use Essential Oils

Bathing

Using oils in the bath helps unlock congested pores, eases muscle tension and fatigue, quiets the mind and calms the spirit. After running a warm bath, add eight to ten drops of your chosen oil and relax in the bath for at least ten minutes.

Suggested bath oils are: bergamot, chamomile, frankincense, geranium, jasmine, lavender, mandarin, neroli, rose, tangerine, ylang ylang. Add vegetable oil for dry skin.

Bath Therapy

Put seven drops from a flower essence or essential oil bottle in bath water in the morning, before noon. For best results soak for 30 minutes. Water is a conductor for electrical force. It activates the aura, cleanse the energy fields and releases karmic patterns.

Massage

Choose specific oils to suit the condition and temperament for the massage. Add ten to twelve drops to one ounce of massage oil.

Inhaled as a vapor

Two to three drops. Put hot water into a bowl, add the oil, cover your head with a towel and lean over and inhale. Breathe deeply.

Diffusers – Use candle or electric diffusers. These diffusers should be made out of clay or glass.

Humidifiers – Add one to nine drops to the water.

Room Sprays – Four or more drops, per one cup of water.

Recipe for Essential Oil Blends

20 to 60 drops base oil per 100ml.
5 to 15 drops essential oil per 25ml.
2 to 3 drops per teaspoon.
Or 25ml (12-13 drops per 1 fluid ounce base oil)

Vaporization / Inhalation

Inhale the essential oil by putting six to seven drops onto a tissue; take deep breaths for maximum benefit.

Anointing

Use myrrh, frankincense, jasmine, rose, lavender on the third eye along with soul affirmation.

For protection use rosemary, juniper and vetiver. Put on solar plexus and move energy counterclockwise. It is wonderful to use specific oils on the chakras, and the areas of the body that need attention.

Oils for Meditation Burners and Diffusers

Angelica – connects with the divine
Frankincense
Juniper – a psychic cleanser
Lavender
Rose
Rosemary – for spiritual protection
Rosewood
Sandalwood

Oils for Specific Ailments

Over-thinking and Worry: Sandalwood, lemon, frankincense, myrrh

Depression, Fear and Nervous Tension: Chamomile, orange, bergamot

Disempowerment and Indecision: Ginger, juniper

Clarity of Mind: Rosemary

Anger and Frustration: Orange, bergamot, grapefruit, peppermint, chamomile, yarrow, lavender, oil of rose, bergamot

Impatience and Intolerance: Bergamot, lavender, peppermint

Mental Fatigue: Rosemary, tea tree, laurel

Tension and Agitation: Chamomile, sweet orange, bergamot

Relaxation and Rejuvenation: Frankincense, lemon and peppermint

Anxiety and Apprehension: Basil, bergamot, clary sage, frankincense, geranium, grapefruit, jasmine, juniper, lavender, neroli, orange, patchouli, rose, sandalwood, vanilla, verbena, vetiver, ylang ylang, thyme, geranium

Nerves: Angelica, basil, bergamot, camphor, cypress, jasmine, lavender, melissa, neroli, patchouli, chamomile, rose, rosewood, sandalwood, tangerine, vetiver, ylang ylang

Lack of Confidence and Self-esteem: Rosemary, jasmine, rose

Low Morale: Thyme, pine, cedarwood

Lack of Self-worth: Rose, jasmine

Anxiety and Depression: Lavender and rose

Sudden Fear: Geranium, vetiver, rose

Calming: Jasmine, ylang ylang

Vulnerability: Pine and thyme

Resistance to Change: Cypress and juniper

Chronic Indecisiveness: Clary sage, bergamot, orange

Frustration and Negativity: Bergamot, orange, neroli

Bitter: Chamomile, bergamot

Lonely and Forlorn: Marjoram, rosemary, myrrh

Oils for Specific Ailments – continued

Over-attachment: Frankincense and myrrh

Joylessness: Jasmine, ylang ylang, orange

Depression: Basil, bergamot, camphor, chamomile, clary sage, geranium, grapefruit, Jasmine, lavender, neroli, patchouli, rose, sandalwood, ylang ylang

Abandonment: Rose, neroli, ginger

Sudden Fear: Geranium, vetiver, rose

Nervous Tension: Chamomile, orange, bergamot, lavender

Chakra Fragrances

Root: Cloves, Cedar, Jasmine, Rose, Patchouli, Myrrh, Musk

Navel: Ylang Ylang, Sandalwood, Jasmine, Rose

Solar Plexus: Peppermint, Lemon, Rosemary, Carnation, Lavender, Cinnamon, Marigold, Chamomile, Thyme, Juniper, Vetiver

Heart: Attar of Roses, Bergamot, Clary Sage, Geranium, Melissa

Throat: Sage, Eucalyptus, Frankincense, Lavender, Sandalwood, Chamomile

Third Eye: Rosemary, Juniper

Crown: Sandalwood, Jasmine, Rose, Lavender, Frankincense

Palm Chakras: Put on center of palms of hands

Foot Chakras: Put on soles of feet

Eight Chakra: Spiritual center, higher self. Spray with a spritzer around top of head. Frankincense, Lavender, Neroli, Angelica

Essential Oils

Angelica: Supports and connects the energy fields with the soul. Opens intuition and helps one realize deep inner self. Puts one in touch with angelic realms, enhances meditation. Detoxifies the body, rebuilds vital force. Good for headaches and stimulates glandular system.

Bay: Helps heal the heart and throat chakras and the illnesses associated with them. Good for the immune system. Helps heal and balance the lung meridians.

Basil: Cleanses the colon. Antiseptic. Stimulating. Reduces fever and virus. Increases devotion and intuition. Helps with confidence and courage. Helps lift depression.

Bayberry: Used for clearing the astral and mental bodies. Clears the entire auric field. Balances the spleen and heart chakras.

Bergamot: Relaxing. Antiseptic. Stimulating. For courage, harmony. Releases depression, anxiety and anger. Brings more light to situations. Eases tension, worry and anxiety.

Camphor: Opens the mind, senses, and lungs. Increases perception and meditation. Alleviates headaches. Good for devotional ceremonies, brings more light. Good for confidence, discernment. Helps with nervous ailments.

Carnation: Used to increase the metabolic system. Balances and removes negativity in the energy field. Clears and balances the meridians, protects and strengthens the aura.

Cedar: Encouraging, balancing. Helps with anxiety, emotional imbalance, stress. Supports the nervous system.

Cedarwood: Relaxing, aids in diabetes, arthritis, and edema. Good for ai cleaning, harmonizing, opens psychic centers, aggression, anger, dishonesty, fear, bronchitis, urinary tract disorders.

Chamomile: A soothing tonic for nerves and restlessness. Helps support the endocrine system and the kidneys. Releases emotional toxins. Helps calm down the stomach area. Good for indigestion. Excellent to use in calming down children.

Cinnamon: Good for meditation, healing and protection.

Essential Oils – continued

Clary Sage: Eases stomach cramps. Helps weak digestion, bronchitis, asthma, menstrual cramps, PMS, headache, nervousness, paranoia, fear, depression. Brings clarity and balance, eases tension, anxiety, worry and grief. Boosts confidence.

Clove: Very cleansing and antiseptic. Helps strengthen spleen and heart meridians. Used for protection and releases negative energy. Good for eyesight, nervousness, and memory. Strengthens kidneys.

Cypress: Bolsters weak connective tissue. Controls heavy menstruation, bleeding, coughing. Aids concentration, nervous breakdown, squandering energies, uncontrollable sobbing, offers peace and comfort, eases anxiety. Enhances physical vitality.

Eucalyptus: Good for purification, health and vitality, confusion, rage, poor concentration. Healing oil that strengthens and balances all meridians. Used for all respiratory illness and to support the immune system. Balances the heart chakra and releases the pain of the past. Helps with all kinds of disturbing emotions. Cleanses and purifies negative energy from the aura. Helps alleviate grief and anxiety.

Frangipani: Brings light and ease to the aura. Balances the throat chakra. Used for meditation.

Frankincense: Used more commonly in meditation and for all sacred rituals. Cleanses and balances the aura. Purifies emotional and mental patterns. Evokes inspiration, faith, inner strength and stability. Awakens and balances the crown chakra, and base chakras. Promotes deep stillness, peaceful sleep, connection with spirit and inner guidance.

Gardenia: Works with the emotional plane to bring healthy boundaries. Stabilizes and strengthens all emotional conditions.

Geranium: Good for emotional healing. Fresh, harmonious, and healing. Eases depression, emotional imbalance. Strengthens liver. Good for endometriosis. Effective for menopause problems, diabetes, blood disorders and throat infections. A good nerve tonic, works as a sedative. Helps in cases of uterine and breast cancer.

Ginger: Good for detoxifying the physical body, tonic and stimulating. Promotes confidence and courage. Beneficial for colds, throat, fever and aids digestive problems.

Grapefruit: Helps with depression, brings light and vibrant energy into the system. Stimulates and clears the mind, strengthens the physical body, energizes the nervous system, promotes digestion.

Jasmine: Assists in opening the heart and crown chakras and helps to integrate the energy fields. Stimulates creativity and imagination. Inspires grace and brings the essence of peace to one's being. Eases depression. Helps with back pain, frigidity, impotence, joint and muscle pain, depression, fear, low self-confidence, emotional suffering. Can be an antidepressant or aphrodisiac. Heals breast and uterine infections.

Juniper: Protecting, purifying, honoring. For anxiety, stress, fear, and uncertainty. Helps arthritis, poor circulation and indigestion. A blood purifier, juniper promotes well being and inner strength. Clears negative energy and from the environment and the aura. Strengthens the immune system.

Lemon: Energizing, brings vitality to body, mind and spirit. Stimulates clarity of thought. The color yellow strengthens and supports all mental processes. Works to balance the solar plexus chakra and the organs and conditions associated with it. Eases depression, confusion. A tonic for the immune system and nervous disorders. Cleansing and invigorating and balances the meridians. Joyous, purifying, strengthening. Helps with emotional confusion, fragility. Stimulates clarity of thought. A good antiseptic.

Lavender: Awakens the crown chakra, opens one to intuition and guidance, clears negative energy from the aura and the environment, increases peace of mind and emotional balance. Helps to heal inflictive emotions such as impatience, worry and shock. Good for all infections and speeds up healing processes. Treatment for burns and scalds. A natural antibiotic, antiseptic, antidepressant, sedative, and detoxifier. Promotes healing, strengthens the immune system. Stimulates circulation and helps with nervous system. Tranquilizing and good for the nervous system, anxiety, depression, and PMS.

Lilac: Works with the brow chakras to bring clarity. Heals and balances all other chakras. Opens one to the magical aspects of nature such as angels and fairies. Supports memory and intuition.

Lily: Calms heart, nerves and emotions. Good for stomach, lungs and dry cough. Increases faith, devotion and virtue.

Lotus: Calms mind and heart. Affects deep sleep. Increases love, faith, devotion, and compassion. Opens crown and ajna centers. Symbol for self-realization.

Essential Oils – continued

Magnolia: Works with the heart and throat chakra, and the organs associated with them.

Myrtle: For love and beauty. Alleviates despair. Helps with short sightedness, distraction, coughs, colds, infections, bronchitis.

Mint: Stimulating, clears the mind, head and sinuses.

Musk: Heals and balances the root and naval chakras. Strengthens the kundalini flow of energy. Purifies the blood stream. Revives those who are in exhaustion or collapse. Strengthens heart and reproductive system. Awakens the senses.

Neroli: Opens the heart, brings a sense of inner joy, inspiration and creativity. Helps to transcend negative emotions and boosts confidence and self-esteem. Relieves emotional stress, anxiety, headaches, nervous heart, PMS, fear, anxiety, depression, shock, insomnia, subconscious fear, hopelessness. Brings courage.

Orange: Assists the solar plexus chakra and rejuvenates the body-mind system. Promotes mental clarity, and helps to resolve deep emotional issues. Helps to increase confidence, trust and harmonious feelings. Relaxes and calms the nerves. Helps with weak digestion, gall bladder, heart muscle, bladder, kidney disorders, fever, sadness, need for warmth, self-consciousness, anxiety, nervousness.

Patchouli: Awakens the yin, or inactive meridians. Aligns all centers with the heart center. Earthy and peaceful, helps for grounding by strengthening the navel and root chakras. Brings a deep sense of emotional centeredness and stability.

Pennyroyal: Protects the aura. Releases negative thoughts. Strengthens spleen and solar plexus chakra and heals conditions such as headaches, nervous conditions and skin conditions.

Peppermint: Purifies and energizes the environment. Clears the air, helps direct vital energy. Antiseptic, cleansing, and purifying. Stimulates the mind. Helps with fatigue and exhaustion. Good for stomach disorders, asthma and bronchitis. Inspirational and brings energy, enthusiasm and joy of life, awakening the inner child. Releases negative thinking in the aura and environment. Clears the mind, stimulates thinking and perception and aides in discernment. Good for the body, mind, and spirit. Excellent for headaches and stomach disorders and helps to support the immune system. A natural stimulant.

Pine: Healing, energizing, protecting, good for general fatigue, poor circulation and respiratory tract infections.

Rose: Works to heal and balance the heart. Helps bring about love and healing with the crown and heart chakras. Works to increase the vibration of love.

Rosemary: Balances the solar plexus chakra and heals unresolved emotions. Stimulates brow and crown chakra. Brings clarity to the mind. Stimulates brow and crown chakra. Antiseptic, stimulating. Benefits blood, heart, circulatory system and helps headaches and emotional tension. Promotes menstruation.

Rock Rose: Fights infections, speeds healing of wounds. Good for chronic skin orders, eczema, psoriasis, cystitis, menstrual cramps, and swollen lymph glands. Soothes emotional coldness and emptiness.

Sage: Cleanses; protects; awakens intuition. Releases toxins and tension in the body. Balances the heart and solar plexus. Overall tonic.

Sandalwood: Enhances healing on all levels. Open palm chakras for healing. Brings connection with spirit and increases concentration. Relaxing. Antiseptic. Good for heart and lungs. Cleanses kidneys, reduces fever, irritability and anxiety. Promotes meditation.

Tangerine: Good for second chakra, helps one to open and receive love and strengthen relationships. Assists one in adapting to changes. Relaxes nervous tension, good for massage or bath.

Tea Tree: Speeds up all healing processes. Provides protection, courage, health, strength. Alleviates exhaustion and fatigue. Good as an immune stimulant, antiseptic, antiviral, antibacterial and antifungal. Useful for many conditions, such as candida, infection, ringworm, sunburn, acne, athlete's foot and toothaches.

Thyme: Excellent for the immune system. Activates the thymus gland. Is calming and relaxing. Good for the lung meridian. Balances the third eye and crown chakras.

Tuberose: Healing fragrance for the crown chakra. Good for all meridians. Brings peace of mind and relaxation to all areas of the body and mind. Helps strengthen the emotional body. Increases inspiration and intuition. Good for love relationships.

Vetiver: Oil of tranquility. Brings a deep sense of inner stability. Helps with grounding and feeling connected to inner earth. Calms extreme nervousness and is good for stress, disconnectedness, anorexia and depression.

Violet: Helps to relieve pain. Balances stomach meridian and bladder. Heals and balances the solar plexus chakra. Used in bathing for creating a sense of well being.

Essential Oils – continued

Wintergreen: Works with the spleen, solar plexus and heart chakras to promote healing, aligning all the energies together. Brings a positive attitude towards oneself and promotes health on all levels.

Wisteria: Brings good vibrations. Opens the heart and throat chakras. Strengthens the will and the immune system.

Yarrow: Good for confusion, depression, ambivalence, menopause, meditation.

Ylang Ylang: Helps to overcome sexual issues. Inspires creativity and appreciation of beauty, opens the heart and calms the nerves. Helps release negative emotions. Good for high blood pressure, PMS, fear, rage, anger, low self-esteem, impotence, nervous depression and nervous headaches.

I wearied myself searching for the friend with efforts beyond my strength
I came to the door and saw how powerfully the locks were bolted.
And the longing in me became that strong, and then I saw I was gazing from within the Presence.
With that waiting, and in giving up all the trying, only then did Lalla flow out from where I knelt.

Lalla – Naked Song
By Coleman Barks

Healing Oils and Their Uses for Specific Symptoms

Symptoms	Essential Oil	How used
Aches and pains	Lavender, Myrrh, Cinnamon, Basil, Sandalwood	Massage, bathing, inhalation
Antibacterial	Sandalwood, Myrrh, Jasmine, Gardenia	Massage, bathing, inhalation
Congestion	Eucalyptus, Sage, Basil, Mint	Inhalation
Depression	Lime, Basil, Jasmine, Thyme, Rosemary, Bergamot, Orange, Patchouli, Saffron, Ylang Ylang, Sandalwood	Massage, bathing, inhalation
Digestion	Cardamom, Cloves, Fennel, Ginger	Inhalation
Fatigue	Basil, Cloves, Marjoram, Lavender	Massage, bathing, inhalation
Gynecological disorders	Rose, Lemon, Rosemary Geranium Rose	Massage, bathing, inhalation
Infections	Eucalyptus, Cedar	Massage, bathing, inhalation
Immune functions	Myrrh, Frankincense, Rose, Lotus	Massage, bathing, inhalation
Insomnia	Marjoram, Lavender, Ylang Ylang, Chamomile, Sandalwood,	Massage, bathing, inhalation
Stress, tension	Rose, Lavender, Sandalwood, Basil, Geranium, Neroli, Clary Sage, Lily, Lotus, Frankincense	Massage, bathing, inhalation

Color Healing

History

Since the beginning of human life we have been exposed to color. The ancient cultures of Egypt used color rooms with light that refracted through colored gemstones for healing. East Indian culture used colored gemstones prescribed by Ayurvedic medicine, sometimes using pulverized gemstones in therapies.

European culture used the doctrine of four humors from the Greco-Renaissance periods. Each humor was assigned a color: red for blood, black and yellow for bile, and white for phlegm. The Chinese compiled the Nei Ching medicine text, which records color diagnosis, over 2000 years ago.

The Importance of Color

Color is a great cosmic force and power that influences us on a deep cellular level. Color affects every aspect of our lives and dominates our senses even if we are blind. It gives us information about the environment and affects our mental and physical well being. Mentally, it affects our perception of heat and cold, physically it affects our large and small muscle activity and also our blood pressure, respiration and heart rate.

Each color has seven intrinsic elements.
1. Color manifests in the physical world.
2. Color gives life essence or soul power.
3. Color heals the emotional and mental energy fields.
4. Color unifies and harmonizes.
5. Color is deeply healing and transforming.
6. Color opens the third eye, bringing inspiration and intuition.
7. Color is nature's instrument for spiritual or higher consciousness.

Application of color healing takes in the essence of color and releases discordant energy. It is a powerful tool when working with energy field healing. The aura holds the colors of the seven rays, the spectrum of our universal energy.

Red represents the body and sexuality.

Orange represents the life force or metabolic body.

Yellow represents the solar plexus and emotional energies.

Green represents ego and the connections between the ego and higher self.

Turquoise represents the higher mental or spiritual self.

Blue represents the causal body and motivation.

Violet represents the higher self.

Magenta represents the spirit self and the eternal being.

Color Healing, The Aura and Chakras

The aura and chakra energies work together to create and maintain life. There are seven colors that correspond to the seven chakras.

Red: Base chakra, relates to passion, life energy, sexuality and creativity.

Orange: Sacral (adrenals) relates to physical movement, etheric health, well being and joy.

Yellow: Solar plexus (nervous system) center of recognition and self-worth.

Green: Heart, relates to love, harmony and balance.

Blue: Throat, thyroid, relates to creative expression through sound, communication and truth.

Violet: Third eye (pituitary gland), relates to creative visualization. Gathers instruction from higher self.

Magenta: Crown (pineal gland), relates to the eternal, spiritual self, connects us to cosmic consciousness.

Color Therapies

There are many methods of color therapy used to promote healing and transformation. Color can profoundly affect the energy fields. Each color of light has its own wavelength and specific energies. For example, blue is peacemaking, yellow is up-lifting, red can spark positive action and green stabilizes and centers our energy as well as improves self-esteem.

A variety of methods can be used to infuse the energy field with the healing color that is most strengthening such healing with colored water, colored glasses, colored crystals and color essences.

Methods of Treatment

Color infused water

Colored water may be held or applied to the body to uplift, heal and balance the energy fields.

Color Slides or Colored Glasses

Color slides can be used, along with a penlight, to apply color to the area needing attention.

Colored Lamps

Colored light rays are focused on the body, especially on the back, along the spine and nervous system. Applying color through a color-healing lamp helps rejuvenate the cells of the system. The color permeates the cells of the body.

Color Breathing

Vital energy (or prana) introduced to the body with color breathing, is a powerful tool for healing. Color healing is done with deep rhythmic breathing along with visualizations. The universal life spirit is always available through the breath, bringing power and transformation to the energy fields.

Color Breathing Meditation

To work with color breathing, simply begin at the root chakra and breathe in the color red along with the affirmation that feels right for that chakra. See chakra charts for suggested affirmations. Then move up through the chakras with the breath and the related color. This exercise is very healing and energizing.

Radiate Color Healing Light

The recipient of this healing light sits comfortably. A few moments of breathing and affirmation will set the tone for this session. The healer stands in front of the person and concentrates on the color that the person needs. An affirmation can be shared here, such as "I consciously send blue to this person," or, "I transmit blue, calming energy to restore his/her energy fields to peace and harmony."

Color Charged Cloths

Take a piece of colored cloth or silk the size of a postcard and lay it on the area of the body or chakra that needs the particular color remedy. (See color chart for guidance.)

Colors and Their Healing Properties

Colors are absorbed through the eyes and skin; they energize the nerves and stimulate the mind. To stimulate mental fire, use bright colors; to calm use blue. White or blue reduces; green heals and balances. Colors provide emotional strength and can facilitate creativity. Psychological disease can be healed through color and it also stimulates digestion, circulation, improves vitality, increases overall physical activity and energizes the blood. Gems and colored lamps strengthen the aura and the astral body. Color also affects the mind. The astral plane is constantly changing according to the emotions and feelings, and therefore has within its realm a wide variety of colors, thoughts and desire patterns. Colors are an important tool in diagnosing the psychological condition of a person and assists in the understanding of emotions and thought patterns within the aura.

The energy fields appear to be composed primarily of energy expressing itself as color. The shade of color that dominates the chakras and subtle bodies are an indication of an individual's health. The aura consists of seven layers of colored light that surround the physical body of an individual; the vibrations of light and color represent the total makeup, the etheric body, emotional field, mental field and spiritual field.

Red: Brings strength and courage, releases negativity and generates vitality. It also strengthens the life force, will and sexuality, increases circulation and overall energy. Increases the metabolism, strengthens the blood, stimulates and warms the body. It awakens physical life force and is used to clear any disease or illness of the body. Too much red can over stimulate. It is considered the "great energizer" because of the effect it has on the physical constitution. It corresponds to the root chakra, giving vitality and strong creative energy to the body. Treatment with red stimulates the root chakra, releasing adrenaline into the bloodstream, and can reverse dormant or sluggish conditions. Spiritually, red strengthens willpower and creates courage.

Orange: The healing energy of purification strengthens the etheric body, helps all muscular systems, creates harmony in one's sense of self, increases wisdom and creativity. Assists any imbalance of the spleen, pancreas, stomach, intestines and adrenals. It also helps with food assimilation and depression and revitalizes the entire physical body. Orange stimulates the etheric, removes congestion and increases the flow of prana. It brings joy and happiness to one's being, affecting the health aura and creating a balance between the physical and mental bodies. Orange is an energizer bringing creative energy to the body. Called the "Wisdom

Ray," orange works to heal the physical with vitality, at the same time cultivating inner wisdom. It controls the second chakra and assists it in assimilation, distribution and circulation of prana.

Yellow: Brings wisdom, opening the mind to expanded consciousness. It is good for intellectual development, strengthening of the mind and awakening the left hemisphere. Yellow calms the solar plexus, brings positive energy, awakens confidence and optimism and helps heal the stomach, gall bladder and entire elimination system. It is effective in the treatment of headaches and a help in learning. Yellow rays have magnetic qualities and are awakening, inspiring and vitally stimulating to the higher mental body. It is the color of searching for the wisdom of God.

Green: Brings nurturing, harmony, beauty and healing. Strengthens the heart chakra, heals emotional pain, neutralizes nervous energy, calms, soothes and brings balance and healing to the body, mind and spirit. It is good for healing and visualization with the breath, brings abundance and prosperity, promotes growth. Green helps things grow, so one must be careful how it is used in healing. Green brings compassion, peace, soothing, faith, peace and hope as well as relaxing the mind and healing the nervous system. Due to a general healing effect, green is used for inflammation and fevers. Green indicates harmony and balance of the mind and body. It also stimulates the heart chakra. It is a combination of yellow (wisdom) and blue (truth), and has a healing and rejuvenating nature.

Rose: Acts upon the nervous system. Vitalizes and removes depression, symptoms of debilitation. Increases the will to live and helps depression.

Blue: Opens the throat chakra, brings a clearer way of communication and expression of truth, is used to increase creativity and self-expression. Instills self-confidence and connection with inner wisdom. Used in meditation, the color blue brings peace and calmness, enabling devotion, prayer and spiritual healing. Helps with the respiratory system and ear, nose and throat conditions. It also calms energy imbalances and helps reduce high blood pressure. Works well with children's diseases. Awakens intuition, self-expression, and inspiration. The color of truth, perfection and devotion, blue is related to the throat chakra, which is considered the greatest creative center in the body and brings calm and peace of mind.

Indigo: Brings deep inner wisdom, opens one's intuition, connecting with the inner teacher. Assists one to express inner knowing, reveals the mystical nature of life. Indigo indicates devotion and clear, logical thought. Related to the ajna chakra it deals with expansion of consciousness.

Violet: Penetrates negative energy and releases it, opening one to experience total transformation and connection with the divine in life. Helps release stress and brings balance and healing to all conditions. Helps balance the crown chakra prompting purification on all levels. Brings inspiration and humility, balancing the physical and spiritual worlds. Violet rays increase the effect of meditation tenfold and inspire.

Pink: Healing vibration opening one to the gifts of spirit. Pink within the aura denotes a quiet and refined person who likes a peaceful life.

White: Offers protection, strengthens and purifies the entire energy system. Beginning and ending color therapy with white amplifies the effect of other colors. Purifies the mind for serenity and peace.

Black: For protection, grounding strengthening.

Aqua: Used for all healing. Sedates the system and helps calm all aspects of the body and mind.

Brown: Grounds and stabilizes.

Gold: Strengthens and amplifies. Awakens inner healer.

Silver: Increases intuition and balances female and male energies.

Essence is emptiness, everything else accidental
Emptiness brings peace to loving,
Everything else, disease.

In this world of trickery
Emptiness is what your soul wants.
      Rumi

Chakra Healing with Color

Root Chakra

Stimulated with Green, Indigo and Violet.
Soothed by Red, Orange, Yellow and Blue.
Red – Life, physical self, physical plane.
Energizes vitality, creativity, power and courage. Stimulates nerves.

Navel Chakra

Stimulated by Red.
Calmed by Blue, Yellow.
Orange – Health, vital self, physical plane.
Healing, wisdom, circulates prana, strengthen etheric.

Solar Plexus Chakra

Stimulated by Red, Orange, Yellow, Violet.
Calmed by Blue and Indigo.
Yellow – Wisdom, emotional plane, power self, self-awakening, inspiring, stimu-
lating, wisdom, digestive process, increases intellect and power of reason.

Heart Chakra

Stimulated by Red, Orange, Indigo and Violet.
Soothed by Yellow, Green and Blue.
Green – Energy, healing self, mental plane, whole self, harmony, balance, stimu-
lates heart, releases tension, and negative energies.

Throat Chakra

Stimulated by Red.
Calmed by Blue, Indigo, Green and Yellow.
Blue – Inspiration, peaceful self, mental plane, healing self.
Truth, perfection, devotion, creativity, peace, calming, intuition, connects us with
higher mental body.

Third Eye Chakra

Indigo – Intuition, inspired self, buddhic plane.
Devotion, clarity, expansion of consciousness, cools, strengthens thyroid and
parathyroid. Purifies blood stream, heals emotional plane.

Crown Chakra

Violet – Spiritual power, spiritual self, logoic plane.
Meditation, inspiration. Purifies blood, stops the growth of tumors.

The Healing Power of Crystals and Gemstones

Crystals and gemstones have been used for thousands of years for correcting disorders in the physical body and energy fields. In the past many valuable stones were crushed and reduced to ashes to produce medicines that were ingested orally. Gems may be kept in water so that the water absorbs their vibration and then used as liquid remedies. The healing energy of gems is the energy of white light with specific healing properties. Crystals bring more beauty and light and change the energy of an area. Light reflected off a crystal brings healing and greater harmony. Crystals bring messages of great wisdom as well as energy that heals and transforms. They have the power to receive, contain, project, emanate and reflect vibrations. Through using crystals it is possible to awaken one's dormant energies and remove energy blocks. They also help align the energy fields with the greater universal energy fields. Through this alignment our energy fields are raised to a much higher level and we then develop intuition and a deep connection with the source of life. Crystals are mirrors of our soul and can be powerful tools on our transformation path, reflecting our true nature and our soul's gifts.

Crystals, the most highly evolved in the mineral kingdom are symbols of radiant white light energy. All crystals are expressions of light and energy and each has their own rate of vibration.

Crystals come in seven specific shapes

1. Isometric (cubic) example: fluorite crystals

2. Tetragonal (four sided) example: wolfinite

3. Hexagonal (six sided) example: emerald

4. Triginal (three sided) example: quartz

5. Othorhombic (lozenge shape) example: topaz

6. Monolinic (simply inclined) example: azurite

7. Trilinic (three inclined) example: turquoise

How crystals are used

• As remedies

• Worn as a talisman

• For pendulums

- For laying on of stones

- For meditation

- Can be held or worn to absorb properties

- Can be placed in visual range to aid in focusing

- For aura cleansing and balancing

- In jewelry as an aid in maintaining, mental clarity, improving concentration and emotional stability. Used to clear away emotional debris and to enhance healing abilities.

Care and Cleaning

Place crystals where they can reflect their light and radiate their beauty. Cleanse new stones by soaking in sea salt water for at least three hours.

Recharging

Keep in a well-lighted room.

How to Make Crystal Remedies

Place stones or crystals in pure leaded glass; fill with distilled water. Place in the morning sun for about three hours. The water will be infused with the vibration of the crystal as well as the color of the stone. Put in dropper bottles and test regarding the amount to take, or use approximately 10 drops several times a day.

Suggested stones for remedies: clear quartz, tourmaline, rose, adventurine and amethyst. Stones can also be used with creams or massage oil to enhance the effect of the massage.

Green stones produce a healing affect, red and orange stones a revitalization affect, pink enhances love and heart opening, blue is calming, and violet intensifies the connection with higher consciousness.

Programming Crystals

Thoughts, wishes and blessings can be programmed into crystals. Direct the affirmation or thought into a clear quartz crystal and the crystal will carry the message for you. Crystals will carry out whatever healing intention you might have.

Gems and Balancing the Seven Centers

The seven centers of vital energy receive and transmit energy in the form of color. Their correct functioning depends on both psychological and physical health. Gemstone therapy has a direct action on balancing the subtle energy centers.

To balance the centers with the use of crystals or gems, first detect the center that needs balancing. Then, when the person is lying down in a relaxed state, apply the stones to the center. (See each chakra chart.)

The Crown Center
Rules the pineal gland, brain and right eye; and is balanced by emerald, amethyst, fire agate, labradorite or malachite, diamond, amethyst, clear quartz, crystal, topaz, alexanderite, sapphire and selenite.

The Third Eye Center
Rules the pituitary gland, left eye, ears, nose and nervous system and is balanced by topaz, amethyst, carnelian, emerald, labradorite, malachite, sapphire, lapis, sodalite, quartz and opal.

The Throat Center
Rules the thyroid gland, bronchial and vocal organs, lungs, alimentary canal, and comes into balance through the diamond, amber, aquamarine, citrine, emerald, topaz or turquoise, chalcedony, lapis lazuli, agate, celestite, sodalite and sapphire.

The Heart Center
Rules the thymus gland, heart, blood, vagus nerve, and circulatory system and may respond to sapphire, bloodstone and topaz. Rose quartz, tourmaline, lapis, amber, tiger-eye, topaz, aventurine, azurite, quartz, malachite, and moonstone.

The Solar Plexus Center
Rules the pancreas, stomach, liver, nervous system, and gall bladder and comes into balance with ruby, amber, aquamarine, citrine, emerald, moonstone, pearl and turquoise. Citrine, turquoise, lapis, amber, tiger eye, topaz, aventurine and quartz.

The Navel Center
Rules the reproductive system and comes into balance by the use of pearl, amber, amethyst, aquamarine, carnelian, coral, fire agate, garnet, and labradorite. Carnelian, moonstone, citrine, topaz, coral, and tourmaline.

The Root Chakra
Rules the adrenals, spinal column, and kidneys and comes into balance through coral, garnet, turquoise, agate, hematite, blood jasper, garnet, ruby, bloodstone, smoky quartz, onyx and tiger-eye.

Crystals and Gemstones

Adventurine: Promotes harmony and peace. Calms nerves. Strengthens kidneys, liver, and spleen. Supports throat, solar plexus and heart chakras.

Agates: Grounding stone. Bestows protection. Tones and strengthens body and mind.

Alexandrite: Promotes regeneration. Assists in healing the nervous system, spleen and pancreas. Helps with spiritual transformation.

Amber: Brings harmony to endocrine system. Clears electromagnetic field. Promotes healing and is soothing and harmonizing.

Amethyst: Works with the crown chakra to increase higher consciousness. Good to purify as in the violet ray. Raises the consciousness. Strengthens endocrine and immune systems.

Aquamarine: Calms nerves. Strengthens kidney, liver, spleen and thyroid. Purifies physical body. Good for meditation. Supports throat and solar plexus chakras.

Azurite: Enhances flow of energy through nervous system. Heals mental body. Supports third eye and throat chakras.

Bloodstone: Good for bloodstream.

Carnelian: Balances and energizes kidneys, lung, liver, gall bladder and pancreas. Vitalizes energy field. Supports solar plexus chakra.

Celestite: Reduces stress, brings peace of mind. Good for creative expression.

Clear Quartz: Works to amplify any healing or spiritual intention. Good for meditation. Activates pineal and pituitary glands.

Citrine: Good for communication. Supports the solar plexus and navel chakras.

Copper: Good for blood purification and detoxification. Enhances and is a strong conductor of energy.

Diamond: Magnifies all energy, positive or negative. Supports crown chakra. Aids in alignment with higher self.

Emerald: Tonic for body, mind and spirit. Supports heart, liver, kidneys and the immune system. Aligns energy fields. Enhances emotional body chakra. Supports heart and solar plexus chakras.

Fluorite: Cleanses and refines. Good for healing and meditation.

Garnet: Good for grounding. Brings joy and energy to root, navel and solar plexus chakras. Heals all body systems. Purifies blood.

Gold: Purifies and energizes all systems. Regenerative and restorative. Attracts positive energy into aura. Promotes illumination, love and compassion. Supports navel, heart and crown chakras.

Hematite: Grounding. Disperses negativity. Good for cleansing bloodstream. Energizing and revitalizing.

Herkimer Diamond: Good for meditation. Works with ajna chakra. Clears and balances etheric. Cleanses energy field.

Jade: Strengthens and supports immune system, heart and kidneys. Brings emotional balance and releases negativity.

Kunzite: Opens and supports heart center. Promotes surrender and release. Strengthens cardiovascular system.

Lapis Lazuli: Strong support for thyroid. Enhances psychic abilities and communication with higher self. Supports and energizes the third eye and throat chakras.

Love Stone: Good for circulation. Aids in release of stored emotions. Supports heart chakra.

Malachite: Brings emotional strength.

Moldavite: A deep green stone that fell to earth about 15 million years ago. Opens one to higher self and reception to higher dimensional sources.

Moonstone: Cleansing for the emotional body. Works with ajna chakra. Heals stomach, spleen and pancreas.

Obsidian: Clears fears. Grounds and protects. Heals stomach and intestines. Absorbs negativity.

Opal: Magnifies energy, positive or negative. Relieves stress. Aids in connecting with higher energies.

Pearl: Cleanses and purifies. Brings what is hidden or dark into consciousness.

Peridot: Regenerative powers for all systems of the body. Purifies, balances and tones body and mind. Aligns the energy fields. Stimulates personal growth.

Rose Quartz: Good for the emotional heart. Promotes nurturing, compassion and forgiveness. Assists in healing the kidneys.

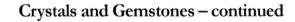

Crystals and Gemstones – continued

Ruby: Grounds and stabilizes. Increases vitality. Protects, clears and restores blood and circulation. Supports root chakra.

Sapphire: Supports throat chakra. Good for creative expression. Strengthens heart and kidneys. Activates pituitary gland.

Silver: Enhances mental function. Strengthens, purifies and cleanses body systems. Good for grounding and centering.

Smokey Quartz: Disperses negativity. Strengthens kidneys and pancreas. Relieves depression. Supports root chakra.

Sugalite: Good for third eye development.

Tiger Eye: Grounding and centering. Good for digestive system, spleen, pancreas, and colon. Supports navel, solar plexus and root chakras.

Topaz: Yellow: Good for intellect. Works to increase concentration. Blue: Good for expression and dreams, for regeneration of the body and for detoxification.

Tourmaline: Provides endocrine support. Aligns energy fields. Aids in release of fear and brings protection. Strong healing stone for all areas.

Turquoise: Calms nervous system. Good for protection.

Chapter Nine:

Energy Wellness Self Care

To live in the known is bondage,
to live in the unknown is liberation.

Nisargadatta Maharaj, **I Am That**

Breathing Visualizations

First, always be willing to let go –

Yogic Breath

Inhale though your nose expanding the abdomen, rib cage and chest. Allow the breath to inflate three dimensionally, the sides, the front and the back of your body. Exhale slowly, through the nose, allowing the chest to deflate, the rib cage to soften and the abdomen to release back to the spine, in that order. This is the basic yogic breath that is used in these visualizations. Keep your breath full, lengthy and smooth and allow your mind to soften into these visualizations.

Connected Breathing

Begin with the full yogic breath. Connect each breath to the next without a pause in between. Bring your attention into any disturbances in your physical, mental or emotional energy fields. Simply allow yourself to breathe into the discomfort, become aware of the sensation. Do this for 10 breaths and then allow your attention to soften into stillness. Notice any changes that might have occurred.

Chakra Cleansing Breath

Begin with the full yogic breath. Inhale and exhale into each chakra beginning with the crown and working your way down. Become aware of which chakras feel over-energized and which chakras feel deficient. Now, begin with the root and visualize a blue, calming energy to reduce the over-energized chakras, or a red, stimulating energy to balance a deficient chakra. Surrender your mind to this healing process. Always give gratitude and seal your intention with an affirmation such as, "I thank the divine healing energy for assisting me to release all disturbed energy from my being."

Breath of Joy

Interlace your fingers and stretch the palms of the hands outward above your head. Inhale, open your chest and arch your back, allowing your head to fall up and back. Exhale; release your arms to your sides. Interlace your fingers behind your back, pull your shoulder blades together and, again, arch your back and allow your chest to open. Inhale and exhale using the full yogic breath. While doing this visualize and feel yourself rooted with the earth. Remember to feel gratitude for your existence. Feel yourself lengthening up and out of the earth and expanding in all directions into boundless space. Release your arms to your sides and feel the light energy that is present. Repeat this three times saying an affirmation similar to this, " I allow myself to feel the joy that is naturally present within myself and send this joy outward to all."

Daily Chakra Meditation

Place your hand, palm towards the body, at a distance that feels right to you. Start with just a few inches and move further away as you can still feel sensation/energy from the chakra, hovering over each chakra as you speak the following affirmations. You can visualize the color of each chakra as you speak/think the affirmation.

1st Root (red): I am eternally secure. My soul exists through all time.

2nd/Navel (orange): I am one with the divine mother. I love unconditionally.

3rd/Solar Plexus (yellow): Power in the center is the core power. I am one with that power and it runs throughout all of my being.

4th/Heart (green or pink): The river of love flows through my heart and then through my whole body. I am a child of love, present, connected and surrendered to the flow.

5th/Throat (light blue): My voice is clear and true.

6th/Third Eye (indigo blue): I see through the illusions to truth.

7th/Crown (gold or violet): I bring all my learning, gifts and tools from all lifetimes as medicine for the greater good.

See AuraTouch (page 176) for an additional method of energy balancing.

Energy Field Protection, Grounding and Clearing

Grounding Energy

Sit comfortably, spine straight, feet flat on the floor, or lie down feet uncrossed. Close your eyes and focus on your lower abdomen. Visualize the root center. See it connected to a cord carrying your energy into the earth. This grounding cord is the channel in which energy flows deep below the earth's surface. Allow the breath to assist in deepening awareness of the moment. Breathe out, releasing all thoughts and emotions. Breathing in, feel a sense of peace and calm. Your sacred cord links you with the source from which you came, the deep silence, the origin of your being. Feel this sacred cord anchor in the earth's core, holding you in the safety of divine light. This cord connects to your foundation, a sense of stability, trust and centering. Use this sacred cord anytime you are in need.

Protection Ceremonies

Breathe deeply and center yourself in your heart. On the inhalation, breathe in a beautiful golden light and surround yourself with this sphere of light as you exhale. Affirm, "I am strong, protected and shielded by divine light."

Shielding Techniques – Use of Energy Shields

Visualize a golden disk, full of light and protection, and mentally place it over the chakras that need protection, especially the solar plexus chakra.

Connecting Heaven and Earth Etheric Energy Flow

Begin with awareness at the crown center. Gently breathe and visualize the breath moving down from the crown center, the third eye center, the throat center, the heart center, the solar plexus center, the navel center and root. With your breath, visualize the colors you need as you bathe in radiant, healing light.

When you feel ready, focus your attention on the foot chakras (soles of feet) and breathe in the energy of Mother Earth through the soles of the feet and up through the chakras, connecting the earth and heaven circles of cosmic energy.

Your Life Essence and Your Connection with Nature

Root Center: Lotus position, connection with earth energy, grounding.

Navel Center: Ocean, waterfalls, streams, lakes, ponds, all water aspects.

Solar Plexus Center: Sun, fire, desert, heat, all warming aspects of nature.

Heart Center: Meadows, forest, gardens, all green aspects of nature.

Throat Center: Water, skies, all blue aspects of nature.

Third Eye Center: Healing through stargazing and night skies.

Crown Center: Healing through climbing to high places, mountains.

Energy Exercises

Cross Crawl

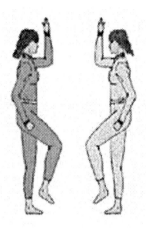

The cross crawl is an excellent exercise to reconnect the energy fields, clearing stagnant electromagnetic energy as well as offering a path to feeling balanced and centered. Use as a daily exercise, before or after a stressful event, to help with learning issues and to help with left and right brain integration. The cross crawl exaggerates normal walking movements, the opposite arm and leg moving together as if marching. Cross crawl can be done standing, sitting or lying down. If unable to exert normal strength, lift the opposite hands and feet, alternately tensing the muscles of the opposing arm and leg pairs, or have someone else lift the opposite arm and leg.

Tibetan 5 Rites

There are seven psychic vortices in the body. Vortex A is located within the forehead. Vortex B is located in the posterior part of the brain, Vortex C is in the region of the neck, and Vortex F and G are located one in either knee. These psychic vortices revolve at great speed.

Rite number one: Stand erect with arms outstretched, horizontal with the shoulders. Now spin around until you become slightly dizzy. There is only one caution; you must turn from left to right (see diagram).

Rite number two: Lie flat on your back on the floor or the bed. Then place the hands flat down alongside the hips. Fingers should be kept close together with the fingertips of each hand turned toward one another. The feet are then raised until the legs are straight up. If possible, let the feet extend back a bit over the body, toward the head, but do not let the knees bend. Then slowly lower the feet to the floor and for a moment allow all the muscles to relax. Repeat.

Rite number three: Kneel on your mat or prayer rug, place hand on the thighs and lean forward as far as possible with the head inclined so that the chin rests on the chest. Now lean backwards as far as possible, at the same time the head should be lifted and thrown back as far as it will go. Then bring the head up along the body, learn forward and start the rite all over.

Rite number four: Sit on a mat with legs stretched out to the front. Then place the hands alongside the body, palms flat on the floor. Now raise the body and bend the knees so that the legs, from the knees below, are practically straight up and down. The arms too, will be straight up and down while the body, from the shoulders to the knees, will be horizontal. Before pushing the body to a horizontal position the chin should be well down on the chest. Then, as the body is raised, the head should be allowed to drop gently back as far as it will go. Next, return to a sitting position and tense every muscle in the body.

Rite number five: Place the hands on the floor with two feet apart. Then, with the legs stretched out to the rear with the feet also about two feet apart, push the body and especially the hips, up as far as possible, rising on the toes and hands. At the same time the head should be brought so far down that the chin comes up against the chest. Next allow the body to come slowly down to a sagging position, bring the head up, causing it to be drawn as far back as possible.

Chakra Exercises

Root Chakra
Exercise

Navel Chakra
Exercise

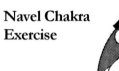

Spleen Chakra
Exercise

Solar Plexus
Chakra Exercise

Heart Chakra Exercise

Third Eye and Crown Chakra Exercise

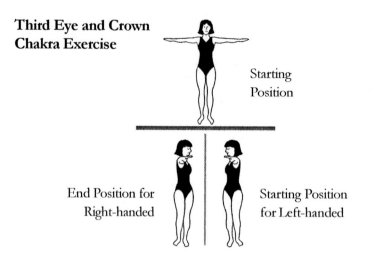

Starting
Position

End Position for
Right-handed

Starting Position
for Left-handed

Cook's Hook-ups

Cook's Hook-ups restores balance to disturbed energy currents. Wonderful for relaxation, concentration, and integration of mind and emotions.

1. Sit comfortably with legs crossed and cross the arms over the chest. Hold this position until you feel complete.

2. Hold finger tips together in a "rainbow arch."

Energy Tune-up for Daily Self-care

The energy tune-up can be used done in about 10 minutes as a quick pick-me-up for clients or for self-care.

1.   Begin the energy tune-up by doing several cross crawls, right leg with left arm, as shown in the Energy Exercises section. You can do this exercise walking or jumping, slow or fast. The cross crawl brings the right and left hemisphere into balance and creates a clear circuit in the energy fields.

2.   Run the energy from your pubic bone to the lower lip. Zip-up! (Creates a strong protective flow.)

3.   Thump on the thymus gland, the area of the chest that the fictitious character Tarzan uses as well to increase strength. The thymus gland assists in overall vital energy and increases brain activity. Also good for waking oneself up if feeling sleepy, unfocused, and unclear in any way.

4.   Rub lymphatic glands in chest area, move hands about 4 inches outside of clavicle and three inches down. Kidney 27 point. This point will assist in bringing energy into the body.

5.   Rub Kidney points in the back of the body; put hands on waist, fingers pointing toward abdomen and thumbs pointing toward the back. Where the thumbs rest is usually where the kidney point is. If it is tender then it needs releasing. Use bending exercise forward and backward to increase the effectiveness of this point release.

6.   Vigorously rub hands along side of outer thighs, from the hip to the knee. These are lymphatic points for the gall bladder and are often very tender. You can use your knuckles for a deeper release.

7.   Run the energy from your head down to the feet and back in a sweeping motion. Work with appropriate affirmation.

8.   Deeply hold the point in the middle of the foot, Kidney 1, known as an emergency revival point. This point helps bring in the vital force and also helps ground displaced energy.

9.   Bring energy from earth, scooping it up and bathing the entire energy field, and then release it to the heavens.

10. Zip up; bring the energy from the pubic bone and the tail bone to the point below the lower lip zipping yourself up in a bubble of healing, white, protective light.

Emotional Freedom Technique

by Gary Free

(See diagram for Tapping Procedure on page 159.)

Offered by permission. Visit www.emofree.com for a complete listing of teaching videos, EFT Certification and more.

Tapping meridian points along with affirmations is an effective way to release stress from the energy fields. The seventeen points offered in the Emotional Freedom Technique will help you release suppressed emotions and beliefs and experience an overall renewal of your life force.

Step One – Dialogue with client to determine emotional or mental stress. Use charts that test strong for further clarity. Rate the disturbance between one and ten. (See guidelines below on how to rate disturbances.)

Step Two – Tap on the meridian points five times using the affirmation below. After you have done this see if the disturbance has subsided.

Step Three – Rate the disturbance again, to determine if it is lessened.

Step Four – If the disturbance remains, tap up to three more times and than rate again.

Step Five – For persistent disruption, tap the points for psychological reversal.

Step Six – Hold neurovascular points while the client does deep breathing and sees the disturbance as if on a movie screen. See the story connected with the disturbance and remain in observation. You may also use the tapping procedure to enhance this powerful technique. Use muscle testing to determine other areas of healing that need attention. Psychological reversals are a disruption in the energy field that could be called the energy culprit. Work with sacred dialogue suggestions to assist in bringing forth any hidden energies.

The Emotional Freedom Technique Opening Procedure

Rate stress level once in the beginning of the session and one or two more times during and at the end. Tapping the acupoints stimulates and changes the body's energy flow, releasing disturbances in the field.

Scale of 1-10 – Zero means that the issue does not bother you and you are neutral and relaxed.

One – Absence of stress

Two – Slight discomfort, mild irritation

Three – Unpleasant feeling

Four – Tolerant of stress, but uncomfortable

Five – Very uncomfortable but not completely out of control

Six – Extremely uncomfortable, life is altered

Seven – Severe emotional pain

Eight – Very disturbed, crisis

Nine – Increasing to almost intolerable

Ten – Extreme Crisis

Important Points to Remember While Tapping:

The Sore Spot

There are two Sore Spots and it doesn't matter which one you use. They are located in the upper left and right portions of the chest and you find them as follows: Go to the base of the throat about where a man would knot his tie. Poke around in this area and you will find a U shaped notch at the top of your sternum (breastbone). From the top of that notch go down three inches toward your navel and over three inches to your left (or right). You should now be in the upper left (or right) portion of your chest. If you press vigorously in that area (within a two inch radius) you will find a "Sore Spot." This is the place you will need to rub while saying the affirmation. This spot is sore when you rub it vigorously because lymphatic congestion occurs there. Rubbing it disperses that congestion. Fortunately, after a few episodes the congestion is all dispersed and the soreness goes away. Then you can rub it with no discomfort whatsoever. To treat psychological reversals, you can tap or rub on the point, clockwise.

The Karate Chop Point

The Karate Chop point (abbreviated KC) is located at the center of the fleshy part of the outside of your hand (either hand) between the top of the wrist and the base of the baby finger or – stated differently – the part of your hand you would use to deliver a karate chop. Instead of rubbing it as you would the Sore Spot, you vigorously tap the Karate Chop point with the fingertips of the index finger and middle finger of the other hand. While you could use the Karate Chop point of either hand, it is usually most convenient to tap the Karate Chop point of the non-dominant hand with the two fingertips of the dominant hand. If you are right handed, for example, you would tap the Karate Chop point on the left hand with the fingertips of the right hand.

The Basic Tapping Sequence

The setup ...

Repeat this affirmation three times while continuously rubbing the Sore Spot or tapping the Karate Chop point:
"Even though I have _____ , (specify energy disturbance) I deeply and completely accept myself."

The sequence ...

Tap about seven times on each of the following energy points while repeating the reminder phrase at each point. (See tapping chart.)

1.   EB = Beginning of the eyebrow. Trauma, frustration, restlessness.

2.   Forehead. Neurovascular points, about halfway between the hairline and the eyebrow, where the indentation on the forehead is, or about one inch up from the eyebrow. (As shown in the description of Emotional Stress Release in this section.) These are strong emotional points to hold, or tap gently while saying affirmations or tapping statements. For Depression, anxiety, trauma, painful memories.

3.   SE = Side of the eye. Anger.

4.   UE = Under the eye. Anxiety, nervousness.

5.   UN = Under the nose. Embarrassment.

6.   Ch = Chin. Shame.

7.   CB = Beginning of the collarbone, anxiety, on the chest, between and slightly down from the collarbone points. Immune system, energy improvement.

8.   UA = Under the arm. Nervousness, self-esteem.

9.   BN = Below the nipple. Where rib cage ends. Important point for sadness and unhappiness.

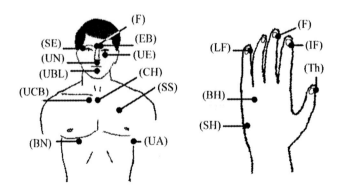

10. Th = Thumb. Helps with tolerance and arrogance.

11. IF = Index finger. Located on either index finger, on the side of the fingernail closest to the thumb. Helps to release guilt.

12. MF = Middle finger. On either middle finger. For treating jealousy, and addictive cravings.

13. BF = Baby finger. Inside tip of either hand, where the fingernail joins the cuticle. Helps to release anger.

14. KC = Karate Chop. Side of hand located on the little finger side of either hand, the palm crease that is closest to fingers. Important point for sadness and psychological reversal.

15. Back of hand. Points between the little finger and ring finger knuckles, in the direction of the wrist. For pain, depression, and loneliness. Important point for psychological reversals.

After performing the tapping sequence above, the next procedure helps the body assimilate the EFT process. This is called the 9 Gamut actions or brain balancer.

 Wherever I shine the lamp light of Divine breath, there the difficulties of the whole world are resolved. The darkness, which the earthly sun did not remove, becomes through My Breath a bright morning.

Rumi (1,1941)

The 9 Gamut actions are:

Tap on the back of the hand between the little finger and ring finger while following the nine steps below:

1. Eyes closed.

2. Eyes open.

3. Eyes hard down right while holding the head steady.

4. Eyes hard down left while holding the head steady.

5. Roll eyes in a circle as though your nose were at the center of a clock and you were trying to see all the numbers in order.

6. Same as item five but reverse the direction in which you roll your eyes.

7. Hum two seconds of a song such as Happy Birthday. This stimulates brain activity.

8. Count rapidly from one to five.

9. Hum two seconds of a song again.

Meditative Point-holding for Emotional Release

At some point you may want to simply hold the tapping points, while saying the affirmations, along with deep breathing. This is an alternative to tapping for times when you may want a more meditative experience. This is wonderful healing technique that is also very effective, calming and balancing.

Psychological Reversal

When the mind and emotions are not in agreement and there is a conflict between the personality and soul, there is most likely a psychological reversal occurring. This is an energy war between mind and heart that creates conflict between actions and thought. For example; you want to be happy but are choosing to be miserable. Maybe you don't feel worthy of what you want from life. When you work on your goal there is always something that blocks you from attaining your goal and you behave in a manner that is self-destructive. These are blind spots that prevent you from seeing and implementing solutions. You know you have the ability to change, but cannot. Energy Reversal occurs due to switched or reversed electromagnetic energies in the meridians due to layering of issues.

To correct this energy disruption, tap the karate chop point approximately five times. This will change the psychological reversal. If it does not, tap up to 15 times. It is helpful to repeat your soul affirmation while tapping these points.

Other corrections for switching are explained in the opening procedure for Life Essence Awakening Analysis, and include Cross Crawl, Cooks Hook Ups, Figure Eights, Zip Ups, Eye Rotations with Affirmations, drinking water, breathing, rubbing Kidney 27 and navel and rubbing above and below the lip and around the navel.

Eye roll

This aspect of the treatment reduces levels of stress through tapping on the back of the hand between the ring finger and little finger while you slowly move your eyes, looking down at the floor then looking up at the ceiling in one continuous circular motion.

Collarbone Breathing Exercise

Place two fingers of your right hand on your right Collarbone Point. With two fingers of your left hand, tap the Gamut Point continuously while you perform the following five breathing exercises:

1. Breathe halfway in and hold it for seven taps.

2. Breathe all the way in and hold it for seven taps.

3. Breathe half way out and hold it for seven taps.

4. Breathe all the way out and hold it for seven taps.

5. Breathe normally for seven taps.

Place the two fingers of your right hand on your left Collarbone Point and, while continuously tapping the Gamut Point, do the five breathing exercises. Bend the fingers of your right hand so that the second joints or "knuckles" are prominent. Then place them on your right Collarbone Point and continuously tap the Gamut Point while doing the five breathing exercises. Repeat this by placing the right knuckles on the left Collarbone Point. You are now halfway done. You complete the Collarbone Breathing Exercise by repeating the entire procedure using the fingertips and knuckles of the left hand. You will, of course, be tapping the Gamut Point with the fingertips of the right hand.

Healing Mudras

Mudra means to seal or lock. These sacred hand positions can be used to bring balance to the body, mind and emotions and are to seal in our intention. In yoga philosophy each finger corresponds to one of the five elements. Each position shows the relationship of the chakras and elements in our hands. The thumb represents the fire element corresponding to the solar plexus chakra and the adrenal glands. The index finger represents the air element and corresponds to the heart chakra and the thymus gland. The middle finger represents the ether element and corresponds to the throat chakra and the thyroid gland. The ring finger represents the earth element corresponding to the root chakra and the sexual glands. The little finger represents the water element corresponding to the navel chakra and the pancreas. In all mudras the fire element, or thumb, must be included.

Prana Mudra

Vital force
Improves energy, circulation, eyesight and general health. Increases vital force, awakens the root chakra. Join the tips of your little finger, ring finger and thumb. Concentrate on your breathing.

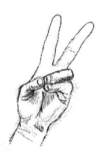

Jnana Mudra

Attaining wisdom
Aids in concentration, meditation, focusing, memory and brain power. Useful for insomnia. Brings a sense of peace and harmony to all aspects of the body and mind. Touch the tip of the thumb with the tip of the index finger, using for any time relaxation is needed. Fingers are pointing upward.

Prithvi Mudra

Increases body energy and flexibility of mind
Opens the mind, assists one to experience bliss, and
balances the nutrients of the body. Helps relieve excess
energy in the root and navel chakras. Touch tip of the
thumb (fire) to the ring finger (earth). Open the rest of the
fingers outward.

Anjali Mudra or Atmananjali Mudra

Prayer
Namaste or Namaskar, meaning
"I salute the divinity within you."
A reverent gesture of respectful greeting. Useful in salutations to another, depicting a great respect. Place your
hands together, palms facing. You can use this hand
position in front of your heart or in front of your third
eye for Namaste salutations and prayer positions.

Apana Mudra

Increases energy
Useful for all water retention problems, helps to
remove toxins from the body. It is a wonderful mudra
to assist in the realization of the self. Join the tip of
the thumb (fire) to the tips of the middle and ring
fingers (sky and earth).

Dhyana Mudra

Meditation
Two hands are open and relaxed with the palms
up, resting on the folded legs, the right hand atop
the left with the tips of the thumbs gently
touching.

Abhaya Mudra

Seal of divine protection

Dispels fear and promotes protection.

Raise your right hand to chest level with palms facing forward. Place your left hand on your left thigh, in your lap or on your heart. Use with mantras, visualizations, prayer, or invocation or with a silent mind.

Concentration: The root chakra (muladhara).

Inhale and fully expand your abdomen. At the same time, raise your hands until they reach your navel again. Coordinate the movement of your hands and abdominal expansion.

Shanti Mudra

Invocation of peace seal

Calms the mind, increases strength and energizes the entire body. Promotes well being.

Sit in a meditative pose. Close your eyes and place your hands on your lap, palms facing up, fingers pointing toward each other. Breathe in, filling your abdomen with air and contracting it. Keep the abdomen contracted and breathe out. Inhale and exhale as deeply as possible.

Concentration: The root center to the navel center. Breathe deeply expanding your chest region by raising your hands to the front of your heart.

Concentration: The solar plexus chakra and the heart chakra. Breathe in and raise your shoulders bringing your hands to the front of your throat.

Concentration: The heart center to the throat center to the third eye center to the crown center. Retaining your breath, spread your arms to the sides, palms facing up. Holding your breath without any strain, stay in this position for a few seconds.

Concentration: The crown of the head. As you exhale, lower your arms to the sides and place your hands on your lap. At the end of your exhalation, contract your abdomen and relax your body. Relax and repeat this mudra exercise, as you desire. Always do deep breathing along with the movement of your arms.

The Healing Power of Sound

Om is the word of creation. In the New Testament (John, chapter 1 verse 1) it is written, "In the beginning was the word and the word was with God and the word was God." The word referred to is *Om*.

The Origin and Nature of Sound

The root chakra is considered the birthplace of sound within our being. Sound travels through the chakras as they are awakened and the highest manifestation of sound occurs in the throat center in the form of Om. In the root center it is expressed as a bird chirping; in the navel center it becomes the twinkling of an anklet; in the solar plexus center it becomes the sound of a bell and then within the heart center it is expressed as the music of a flute.

When the cosmic sound or vibration reaches the throat center it manifests as the cosmic sound, *Om*. The vibration of sound travels along the Sushumna channel, cleansing and re-energizing the karmic patterns of the chakras. Sound evolves from the vibration of the Kundalini Shakti that resides in the base center, into the navel where it is perceived as rumbling. It moves to the heart and is perceived as un-struck. Moving from the heart through the throat it produces all sounds. Para is the highest transcendental state, along with pure energy, Shakti – a divine vibration that unites all. Sound is a direct vehicle to access Parashakti, our highest force. Sound meditation, or japa, is the art of using sound to transcend consciousness to the highest level of divine expression. The power of sound is a direct way to self-realization, clearing the mind of the clutter of thoughts, emotions and impressions. When the mind is in its natural, pure state it reflects the pure consciousness of the infinite.

The use of healing sounds that are expressed with the intention of clearing stagnant energy will bring the higher aspect of truth, divine will and the essence of love and peace into our consciousness. When we use our voice to access divine healing energy through mantras and healing sounds we are able to bring all aspects of our being into alignment with these energies. Through the use of healing sounds we learn to hear intuitively and quicken the development of our higher faculties. Healing sounds are nature's medicine to bring our minds into a state of peace, focus, clarity and attention to the sacred in life. By way of the voice we are able to awaken our life force. Our divine consciousness resonates throughout our being and to the beings of the entire world. The awakening of the life force within keeps the mind still and turned inward to the sacred heart.

The Vedas state that creation arises from the first sound of the universe. *Aum (Om)* is the primal sound, which emanated with the first of creation. *A* represents the material universe, the waking state, *U* represents the astral plane – the dreaming state, which includes the emotional and mental aspects of our natural plane, and *M* represents the experience that lies above the mind and deep-sleep state. *Aum* signifies the three periods of time, the three states of consciousness and all of existence The *OM* sound is represented by these symbols: the three is the material world. The dot or bindu is the absolute consciousness, encased by the veiling power of mind and body. The crescent sign is the deep sleep subconscious where one holds the knowledge and impressions received from previous incarnations. The *OM* sound has three aspects representing Brahma, Vishnu and Shiva. The three aspects also represent the trinity of the Godhead. These three aspects are embedded in the letters of *A, U, M.* The sound *A* arises in the throat, the *U* arises from the tongue and *M* arises from the lips; when they join they become *OM* which arises from the navel. It covers the whole field of the vocal organs, thus *OM* represents all languages and the world. The navel is compared to the lotus and is the place where the life force resides. When *OM* is pronounced it should appear as if a plane is coming from a distance, then drawing closer and closer to us and eventually flying from us. Saying the mantra *OM*, will rejuvenate the nervous system, bring peace and balance to the body, mind and emotions.

Healing Prayers, Sacred Chants

Our prayers are our direct communication with the creator. It is the action of our pure hearts and mind to surrender to divine will and receive guidance.

The Great Invocation

From the point of light within the mind of God, let light stream forth into the minds of men. Let light descend on earth. From the point of love within the heart of God, let love stream forth into the hearts of men. May Christ return to Earth. From the center where the will of God is known, let purpose guide the little wills of people: the purpose, which the masters know and serve. From the center, which we call the race of men, let the plan of love and light work out and may it seal the door where evil dwells. Let light and love and power restore the plan on earth.

Prayer of Saint Francis

Where there is hatred let me sow love, where there is injury, pardon, where there is despair, let me sow hope, where there is darkness let me sow light. For behold, the kingdom of heaven is within you.

The Lord's Prayer

The Lord's Prayer is useful to all healing and is a great benefit to alignment of the chakras with the soul.

Our father which art in heaven (the crown chakra) hallowed be thy name (the third eye chakra). Thy kingdom come (the crown and head chakra as well as spiritual chakras above the head) thy will be done (the throat chakra) in earth (the root chakra) as it is in heaven (the crown chakra). Give us this day our daily bread (the root, navel and solar plexus chakras) and forgive us our trespasses (the lower three chakras), as we forgive those who trespass against us (bringing the energy of the earth through the lower chakras transforming it to light and moving the energies through the upper chakras). And lead us not into temptation (the solar plexus chakra) but deliver us from evil (the resurrection of the heart center) for thine is the kingdom (the throat) and the power (the third eye) and the glory, forever. Amen (the crown center).

Divine Invocations

Ask and it will be given to you; seek and you will find; knock, and it will be opened to you. For everyone who asks, receives, and he who seeks, finds, and to him who knocks it will be opened. Matthew 7:7-8

Invocations to the Archangels

Michael, Angel of protection, is a protective force we can call upon to clear the obstacles of darkness and ignorance and remove the veil from our true identities as beings of light. Gabriel, Angel of strength, death, and resurrection. Uriel, Angel of communication, messenger of God. Raphael, Angel of healing.

May Michael be on my right hand, Gabriel on my left, before me Uriel, behind me Raphael and above me the all-pervading Divine Presence.

Divine Affirmations for the Body, Mind and Spirit

When working with divine affirmations it is important to find one that supports the evolving nature of the soul. Divine affirmations help us release old programming by seeing consciousness in its perfection now. Below are some ideas for divine affirmations.

Divine Affirmations for the Body

• I am whole, well and in complete balance with the perfection of nature.

• I am radiant, free and full of vitality.

• I completely let go of all imbalances in my system, allowing my body, mind and spirit to be in perfect balance.

• I let go of all memory held in my body, breathing in the present moment, free from the past. I see now that my body, mind and spirit are in perfect harmony.

• As I inhale, I focus bringing healing light to my pain and discomfort. As I exhale, I let go of all disharmony. I see my self free from pain and imbalance.

• I am not this physical body; I am not my emotions or thought. I am eternal and not bound to these conditions.

• I bring space, awareness and light to my life, knowing my nature is infinite, unbounded consciousness.

Divine Affirmations for the Emotional and Mental Energy Fields

• I transcend all emotions from my ego nature into the pure emotions of love, light and joy that are expressions of my true self residing in my heart.

• I observe all thoughts that come into my pure consciousness while remaining firmly planted in my heart of purity and stillness.

• My compassion understands that my thoughts and emotions are scars from identification with my ego self. I turn my attention to my heart of sacred wisdom and rest.

• I allow nothing to obscure the vision and oneness of my true nature; all that is temporary simply flows through me and out. I am a sieve of discernment and goodness, loving the divine above all.

• I embody the beauty of the universe, completely letting go of all tendencies to create suffering or pain. I offer my life in service to the divine.

• I let go of all feelings of separation as I merge with my divine consciousness of love and truth.

• I hold my true self dear. I have found a precious rare jewel and keep it safe, polished and radiant at all times.

Divine Affirmations for the Spirit

- I am one with the divine, offering my life to service and truth.
- I offer all of my being to the divine, all that is hidden, all that is revealed. I remain open to divine will, surrendering all personal desires.
- I give my life as a garland of roses, each rose being a lesson learned, each rose with the fragrance of purity and the eternal beauty of my soul.
- I surrender all to the divine, allowing space and emptiness to meet life's calling. I humbly await the opportunity to serve.
- The past is completely forgiven for I am born anew in the infinite possibilities of my freedom as pure and divine consciousness.
- I let go of all sorrow and memories knowing that my true reality is found in the timelessness of life, where I remain.

Healing Chants, Mantras and Sounds

In a spiritual context, the throat center is best used for liberation of the personality self. Through saying mantras, prayer and singing sacred chants we are able to achieve the peace, love and God-consciousness that we yearn for. Mantras are powerful invocations to the divine. They work through the vibration of sound and the intention behind them. Through the practice of turning inward into the stillness of our heart, we begin using a mantra or divine affirmation in support of our soul. When identification shifts from ego self to true divine nature a mantra simply assists the focusing of our mind. Through the use of a mantra, or divine affirmation, we are able to direct attention to our ever-present eternal nature, dissolving any sense of separation, opening to the infinite. The mantra or statement of choice is our vital energy (Shakti) expressed as sound, invoking the divine consciousness within our being.

Many of the mantras suggested in this chapter are derived from the Sanskrit alphabet, the language of the divine. The power of a mantra, when applied to a situation, will transform the energy, bringing about a change in reality. The correct sound is like an invocation or divine command that sets the vibrations of the cosmos into motion, attracting the requested result.

The throat chakra is considered the chakra of miracles because the voice is able to transcend outer reality through a simple command. The throat chakra is the center where the voice, when used in relationship to the highest good, can create miracles through commands, prayers and affirmations.

Mantras are very powerful invocations to the divine. They are used for the intent to change and transform energy. The vibrations from a mantra will move energy for whatever purpose or intention. To infuse a mantra with power is to activate vibrational channels that produce altered states of consciousness, which aid in remembering our true nature.

The Gayatri Mantra

The Gayatri is the mother of the universe, the supreme Shakti, and there is nothing she cannot do. Her mantra purifies the mind, destroys pain, sin and ignorance; brings liberation and bestows health, strength, vitality, power, intelligence and magnetic aura. The Gayatri mantra is the essence of Vedanta that sharpens the intellect. The Gayatri has three parts: praise, meditation and prayer. First, the divine is praised and then meditated upon in reverence and then, lastly, the appeal is made to the divine to awaken and strengthen the intellect, the discriminating faculty of man. The Gayatri is the most essential mantra ever known. It is important to recite the Gayatri at least three times a day – morning, noon and evening. The Gayatri dispels the darkness of ignorance and promotes knowledge, wisdom and discrimination. This is a treasure you must guard all your life. It will protect you from harm, wherever you are. The presence of Brahma will descend on you, illumine your intellect and light your path while this mantra is chanted. Gayatri is the Shakti that animates all life.

Gayatri Ancient Meaning and Pronunciation

Om (Aum): Symbol of the Para Brahman, the basis of creation.

Bhur (Bhoor): Bhu-Loka, (physical plane) the earth.

Bhuvah (Bhoo-vah): Antariksha-Loka, (astral) atmosphere.

Swah (Sva-ha): Swarga-Loka (celestial plane) absolute substratum of creation, heaven, beyond the causal.

Tat (Taht): Transcendent Para-atman, that ultimate reality.

Savitur: Ishwara or creator, equated with divine power, contained in the sun.

Varenyam: Fit to be worshiped or adored. We adore the glorious power of the pervading sun.

Bargo: Remover of sins and ignorance, glory, radiance.

Devasya: Resplendent, shining from whom all things proceed, divine radiance, grace of God.

Dhemahi: We meditate.

Dhiyo: Buddhic intellect, understanding. May he enlighten our intellects.

Yo: Which, who

Nah: Our

Prachodayat: Enlighten, guide, impel. May the prayer direct our intellect towards ultimate reality.

(Dhiyo-Yo-Nat Pracho-dayatt)

The Mantra

Om, Bhur, Bhuvah, Swah, Tat, Savitur, Varenyam, Bargo, Devasya, Dhemahi, Dhiyo, Yo, Nah, Prachodayat.

More Mantras for your Sacred Path

Om Gum Ganapatayei Namaha

Om and salutations to the remover of obstacles (Ganapathi) for which Gum is the seed. Ganapathi or Ganesha, the elephant headed deity. Remover of obstacles.

Om Shrim Maha Lakshimiyei Swaha

Om, I invoke the great power of abundance.

Om Ram Ramaya Swaha

A mantra to correct actions on the physical plane.

Om Namo Bhagavate Vasudevaya

Om, the indwelling source within all of life, kindly reveal the truth to me. The indweller is Vasudeva; the soul, which resides in the heart center. This mantra helps you to call on that power within your soul to further your spiritual growth.

Om Shanti, Om Shanti, Om Shanti Om, Om Shanti, Om Shanti, Om

The Great Peace Mantra

Om Mane Padme Hum (Aa-Oo-M Mah-Nee-Pad-May Hoom)

Om – jewel in the lotus; Hum – Harmonizes nerve tissues, clears subtle impurities from the nadis and nerves, empowers all actions on the subtle level, infusing the cosmic life force into the healing process. Male and female energies come into balance.

Om Namah Shivaya, Om Namah Shivaya, Om Namah Shivaya, Shivayah Namah Om

Shiva, lord of ascetics and recluses, is part of the Hindu trinity. Brahma and Vishnu, the other two parts, are associated with creation and preservation. Shiva, the cosmic dancer, presides over the destructive energies, which break up the universe at the end of each age. This is the process of the old making way for the new; in a more personal sense, "I honor the divine within."

Hare Om, Hare Om, Hare Hare Om, Hare Om, Hare Om, Hare Hare, Om

Hare is another name for Vishnu. The aspect that forgives the past actions of those who take refuge in him and destroys their negative deeds. Hare is a redeemer and a guide to personal salvation as well as the world preserver.

Hare Rama, Hare Rama, Rama Rama, Hare Hare, Hare Rama, Hare Rama, Hare Hare, Hare Krishna, Hare Krishna, Krishna Krishna, Hare Hare

Hare is the glorified form of address for calling upon God. Rama and Krishna were two of the best-known and most beloved incarnations of Vishnu. They took human birth on this earth to lead mankind to eternal salvation. This is the maha mantra, the easiest and surest way for attaining God realization in this present age.

Om Sri Ram Jai Ram, Jai Jai Ram Om Sri Ram Jai Ram, Jai Jai Ram

Victory to Rama. Jaya means victory.

Gate Gate, Paragate Parasamgate, Bodhisvaha

Meaning, "Gone, gone, beyond all illusions of the physical plane, on the breath."

Om Tara, Tu Tare, Ture Svaha

Homage to you, Tara, Divine, Radiant Mother of Compassion and Great Protector

The Mantra of the Heart

Gate, Gate, Paragate, Parasamgate, Bodhi Svaha

Gate means gone – gone from suffering to the liberation of suffering, gone from forgetfulness to mindfulness., gone from duality to non-duality.
Parasamgate means gone all the way to the other shore.
Bodhi means the Light of the Mind.
Svaha means the city of joy.

 Don't wait any longer, Dive into the ocean, leave and let the sea be you. Silent, absent, walking an empty road.
Rumi

Healing Sounds, Pronunciation, Meaning and Benefits

Aum / Om: (Rhymes with home) The divine word serving to energize or empower all things, good for the spine and restores and energizes the entire body and mind. Awakens Prana, opens channels, all mantras begin and end with Om. Clears the mind and increases the strength of our immune system. Awakens prana of positive energy and healing.

Ram: ("A" sounds like "a" in calm) Brings in divine protection giving strength, calm, rest and peace. Good for mental disorders, such as insomnia, bad dreams, nervousness, anxiety, excessive fear, and fright. Helps build the immune system.

Hum: (Rhymes with room) Wards off negative influence, which manifests as diseases, negative emotions, awakens the Agni, and increases digestive fire.

Aym: Improves mental concentration, thinking rational powers and speech, awakens and increases intelligence, mental and nervous disorders. Restores speech, communication control of the senses, mind and is the sacred sound of the Goddess of wisdom, Saraswati.

Shrim: Promotes general health, beauty, creativity, prosperity, strengthens overall health and harmony.

Krim: Gives capacity for work and actions, adds power and efficacy, good for chanting while making preparations.

Hrim: (Rhymes with seem) Cleanses and purifies, giving energy joy and ecstasy.

Hraim: (Rhymes with time) Kidney.

Hra: (Sounds like hurray) Continuous long a, strengthens the rib cage purifies the alimentary canal.

Hram: (hraaaammm as in calm) Clarifies lungs, asthma. Restorative.

Hrum: (Rhymes with room) Stimulates liver, spleen and stomach and reduces abdomen.

Sham: Mantra of Peace. Creates calmness, detachment, contentment alleviates mental and nervous disor-

ders, stress, anxiety, disturbed emotions, tremors, shaking nervous system disorders.

Shum: (Pronounced like shoe but shorter vowel sound) Increase vitality, energy, fertility.

Som: (As in home) Increases energy, vitality, joy, delight, creativity; strengthens mind, heart, nerves; is good for rejuvenation and notification.

The Mritunjaya Mantra for Healing

OM TRAYAMBAKAM YAJAMAHE
(Om-Tri-Yam-Bu-Kam)

SUGANDIM PUSHTI VARDHANAM
(Su-Gan-Dim-Pushti-Vard-Han-Am)

URWARUKAMIVA BANDANART
(Ur-Waru-Kam-Iva-Banda-Nart)

MRITYOR MUKSHIA MAMRITAT
(Mrit-Yor-Muk-Shia-Mam-Ri-Tat)
A very powerful mantra or song for the recovery of illness, or to invoke divine healing light.

Chakra Healing Sounds

Root Chakra	LAM
Navel Chakra	VAM
Solar Plexus Chakra	RAM
Heart Chakra	YAM
Throat Chakra	HAM
Third Eye Chakra	KSHAM
Crown Chakra	OM

Your Healing Hands –
AuraTouch and Chakra Balance

AuraTouch™

Open the palm chakras by rubbing your hands together and sensing the energy there. Create an energy ball in which to focus your attention. Hold the palms together two to three inches apart and move them back and forth. When you have your healing vortex ready begin by scanning your client's aura. Move the palms of your hands down the front of the body, asking for information. If your hands feel magnetically drawn to an area, allow them to receive the information. The following guidelines will assist your scanning and reception.

Does it feel hot, congested, tight? Is there pain? These are signs that there is too much energy in a particular area causing and imbalance.

Does it feel cool, weak, loose? Is there a pain in a different part of the body? These are signs that there is not enough energy, which can also be the cause of an energy imbalance. Check for referral pain or related pain located, for instance, in the neck and lower back.

After scanning the aura, go back again and work with what you have perceived. For weak energy, visually bring in more heat through colors of red to orange, directing energy into an area. For excess energy, use your hand to pull energy out of the congested area, visualizing the calming color blue. AuraTouch can be used for the following purposes:

- Scanning for information in an analysis.
- Finding out if there are any cords, tears, congested areas, weak or excess energy areas and where they are.
- Releasing energy built up in an area or strengthening an area.
- Clearing the aura and reconnecting it with divine energies.
- Renewing and rejuvenating the aura through the use of color, sound and projections of white or healing light.

*Late, by myself, in the boat by myself, no
light and no land anywhere. Cloud cover
thick, I try to stay just about the surface. Yet,
I am already under and living with the ocean.*

Rumi

Clearing the Chakras through Your Healing Hands

Our hands are nature's way of giving us the ability to heal, comfort and direct love to areas of physical, emotional or mental pain or discomfort. The palm chakras are often portrayed in images of Christ healing. The palm chakras are given to us for use in helping others or ourselves heal our energy. For review, we open our palm chakras by simply rubbing our hands together and sensing the energy. Create a vortex of healing energy and apply it to the chakras that need healing.

Chakra Kinesiology Test

Please review the Kinesiology testing guidelines before performing this chakra test. When you feel confident in your testing skills you can use Kinesiology to determine which Chakra is in need of balancing. Remember to always ask your client or friend for permission to test

To begin, place your hand over or above the Chakra being testing (see chart below for location of each Chakra). It is not necessary to touch the body. Begin with one hand over the Chakra while the other hand is used to perform the Kinesiology test. First test the Crown Chakra while asking the question; "Is the Crown Chakra balanced?" If the answer is Yes, meaning balanced, the arm will stay strong. If the answer is No, meaning Unbalanced, the arm will go weak. Do this procedure for each of the chakras.

Crown: At the baby's soft spot. Integration, openness, connection.

Third Eye: Between eyebrows. Perception, right understanding.

Throat: At the throat area. Expression of truth, responsibility.

Heart: Between breastbones. Self-love, integration of mind and emotions.

Solar Plexus: Just below rib cage in the abdomen area above the navel. Emotional nature, integration of power.

Navel: Below belly button. Relationships and self-expression in the world.

Root: At the area of the pubic bone, hold hand above pubic area. Security, groundedness, and trusting in life's process.

For clearing the chakras, place your palms above each chakra and move it in a counterclockwise motion. This will remove static energy and clear negative buildup. Flick your hands after the motion to remove the energy or just open your palms upwards towards the heavens and consciously offer it over to spirit to transform or recycle this energy in the highest and best way. After you clear a chakra, move your hand clockwise on the chakra for a longer duration than was used for the counterclockwise movements. The number of these movements depends on how the chakras feel. Listen to your intuition. Clockwise motions can help to open and energize the chakra.

Note: The chakras are tools for transformation. We balance them through a simple clearing motion (as above), use them to gain understanding of our issues, and map our healing course. One may balance them on one level in one session but the imbalance may soon return again until the issue/imbalance on another level/field is healed.

Chakra Emotions

After you have identified which Chakra needs balancing, you can further use Kinesiology testing to identify the emotions that are either balanced or unbalanced in the Chakra charts that follow. When you identify the emotion that needs balancing along with the corresponding Chakra, use affirmations to release them.

For example, Root Chakra: unbalanced, the target emotion is fear.
Affirmation: "I release fear and bring in more trust in my life."
For more advanced work with affirmations and emotions, see *Life Essence Awakening – Energy Field Kinesiology* by Jaya Sarada.

Root Chakra

Balanced

- Trust
- Gratitude
- Life Energy Intact
- Connection with Nature
- Flowing with Change
- Secure

Unbalanced

- Self-centeredness
- Fearful
- Possessiveness
- Non-trust
- Insecurity

Chakra Emotions - continued

Navel Chakra

Balanced
- Harmonious Feelings
- Sexual Expression
- Creative Life Force
- Considerate and Friendly
- Happily Connected To Life
- Vital Force Balance
- Good Self Esteem

Unbalanced
- Unhealthy Sexuality
- Loss of Innocence
- Cannot Express Feelings
- Suppress Needs and Desires

Solar Plexus Chakra

Balanced
- Feelings of Inner Peace
- Deep Reverence
- Gratitude
- Express Positive Energy
- Sense of Wholeness
- Acceptance of Others

Unbalanced
- Aggressive
- Boisterous
- Manipulative
- Opinionated
- Judgment
- Ego Position
- Self-centered
- Low Self-esteem
- Power Issues
- Distrust
- Insecurity

Heart Chakra

Balanced
- Harmonious
- Surrender
- Tolerance
- Unconditional Love, Forgiveness
- Childlike
- Open Channel
- Radiate Love
- Sincerity
- Compassion
- Wholeness
- Non-judgmental

Unbalanced
- Self-centered
- Intolerance
- Ungiving
- Non-receptive
- Judgmental
- Non-acceptance
- Unforgiving
- Uncaring
- Lack of Self-love

Chakra Emotions - continued

Throat Chakra

Balanced

- Expresses Feeling and Truth
- Inner Knowing
- Attending to Silence
- Honesty
- Truthful Speech
- Creativity
- Listening

Unbalanced

- Thoughtless Actions
- Judgment of Self and Others
- Afraid of Silence
- Not Able to Be Alone
- Manipulative
- Self Expression Blocked
- Offensive Voice

Third Eye Chakra

Balanced

- Clear Perception
- Non-duality
- Clarity
- Intuition
- Reception
- Awareness
- Connected to Source
- One-pointed, Mindful

Unbalanced

- Overly Intellectual
- Rational
- Inability to Integrate
- Too Mental
- Non-perceptive

Crown Chakra

Balanced

- Integrated
- Open to Divine
- Surrendered
- Knowledge of Unity
- Self Reflective
- Masterful
- Integrated
- Whole

Unbalanced

- Frustrated
- Depressed
- Psychotic
- Depressed
- Confused
- Out of Touch With Self
- Anxious
- Fearful
- Not Grounded

Resources and Recommended Readings

Bibliography and Recommended Reading

Anodea, Judith. Wheels of Life. 1987, Llewellyn Publications, St. Paul, MN.

Bailey, A. A. Esoteric Psychology. vol. l, 1936. Reprint. Lucis Publishing Company, New York, 1975.

Bailey, A. A. Esoteric Psychology. vol. 2, 1942. Reprint. Lucis Publishing Company, New York, 1975.

Bailey, A. A. A Treatise on Cosmic Fire. 1925. Reprint. Lucis Publishing Company, New York, 1974.

Bailey, A. A. A Treatise on White Magic. 1934. Reprint. Lucis Publishing Company, New York, 1974.

Bailey, A. A. Esoteric Healing. 1953. Reprint. Lucis Publishing Company, New York, 1977.

Benor, Daniel. Consciousness Bioenergy and Healing, Wholistic Healing Publications. 2004.

Benor, Daniel. Spiritual Healing Scientific Validation of a Healing Revolution. Vision Publications, 2001.

Blavastsky, H.P. The Secret Doctrine. 1988. Reprint. Theosophical University Press, Pasadena CA, 1977.

Brennan, Barbara Ann. Hands of Light: A Guide to Healing through the Human Energy Field. New York, Bantam 1993.

Brother, David Steindl-Rast. Gratefulness, the heart of prayer – an approach to life in fullness. 1984, Paulist Press, Ramsey NJ.

Bruyere, Rosalyn L. Wheels of Light – A Study of the Chakras. Fireside. Simon and Shuster, 1994.

Choa Kok Sui. Miracles through Pranic Healing. 1996 Sterling Publishers, Ltd. New Delhi, India.

Choa Kok Sui. Pranic Psychotherapy. 1989, Sterling Publishers, New Delhi.

Clifford, Terry. Tibetan Buddhist Medicine. 1984 Samuel Weiser.

Davis, Patricia. Subtle Aromatherapy. 1991, The DW Daniel Company Limited, Great Britain.

Dossey, Larry. Healing Words. San Francisco, Harper Collins, 1993.

Eden, Donna. Energy Medicine. 1998, Tarcher/Putnam, New York.

Emoto, Masaru. Hidden Messages in Water. Beyond Words Publishing, 2004 (www.hado.net).

Epstein, Gerald. Healing Visualizations: Creating Health Through Imagery. New York, Bantam Books 1989.

Gerber, Richard. A Practical Guide to Vibrational Medicine: Energy Healing and Spiritual Transformation, Quill, 2001.

Gerber, Richard MD. 1988, Vibrational Medicine. Bear & Company, Santa Fe, NM.

Gerber, Richard MD. Vibrational Medicine for the 21st Century. Harper Collins, Publisher New York, New York, 2002.

Hodson, G. The Seven Human Temperaments. 1952. Reprint. Theosophical Publishing House, Adyar, India, 1981.

Hunt, Roland. The Seven Keys to Color Healing. 1971, Harper and Row, New York, New York.

Hunt, Valerie V. Infinite Mind: Science of the Vibrations of Human Consciousness. Malibu Publishing, 1998.

Jagadish. Nature's Way, A complete guide to health through yoga and herbal remedies. 1999, Times Book International, Singapore.

Jurriannse, Aart. Bridges. 1985, Sun Center, Cape South Africa.

Karp, Reba Ann. Edgar Cayce: Encyclopedia of Healing, 1986.

Kilner, Walter. The Human Aura. 1965 University Books, Inc.

Krishnamurti, J. The Book of Life. Daily meditations with Krishnamurti. 1995, Harper Collins, New York, New York.

Lama Surya Das. Awakening the Buddha Within. 1997, Broadway Books, New York, NY.

Lansdowne, Z. The Rays and Esoteric Psychology. 1989. Samuel Weiser, Inc., Box 612, York Beach, ME 03910.

Leadbeater, C. W. The Chakras. 1987. Reprint. Theosophical Publishing House, Wheaton, IL 60187.

Leadbeater, C. W. Man Visible and Invisible. Quest Books.

Lewis, Den. The Tao of Natural Breathing. 1998, Full Circle Publishers, Delhi, India.

McGarey, William A., M.D. The Edgar Cayce Remedies, 1983.

Mookerjari, Ajit. Kundalini Arousal of Inner Energy. 1982 Thames and Hudson, LTD, London.

Motoyama, Hiroshi. Theories of the Chakras. 1981, Quest Books.

Myss, Caroline. Anatomy of the Spirit. 1996 Crown Publishers.

Natarajan, A.R. A Practical Guide to Know Yourself, Conversations with Ramana Maharshi. 1993 The Ramana Maharshi Center, Bangelore India.

Nisargaddatta Maharaj. Consciousness and the Absolute –The final talks of Sri Nisargadatta Maharaj. Edited by Jean Dunn, 1994, The Acorn Press, PO Box 3279 Durham, NC 27715-3279.

Oschmann, James L. Ph.D., Pert, Candace Ph.D.. Energy Medicine: The Scientific Basis of Bioenergy Therapies. Churchil Livingstone, 1st ed. 2000.

Pandit, M.P. Kundalini Yoga. Lotus Light Productions, Twin Lakes, WI.

Powell, A.E. The Causal Body. 1972. Reprint. The Theosophical Publishing House LTD, 68 Great Russell Street, London, WC1B3B.

Powell, A.E. The Etheric Double. 1983. Reprint. Theosophical Publishing House Ltd., London.

Powell, A.E. The Mental Body. 1986. Whitefriars Press, LTD. London.

Powell, A.E. The Astral Body. 1987. Reprint. Theosophical Publishing House, Wheaton, IL 60187.

Pundit, M. P. Kundalini Yoga. 1993 All India Press, Pondicherry.

Sarada, Jaya: The Path of Return. Grace Publishing, 2001.

Sarada, Jaya. Trust in Yourself – Messages from the Divine. 1988, Grace Publishing.

Sarada, Jaya. The Path of Return –The Light of Parashakti. 2001, Grace Publishing.

Saraydarian, T. The Psyche and Psychism. Vol 1 & 2. 1981. The Aquarian Educational Group, P.O. Box 267 Sedona, AZ.

Simpson, Liz. The Book of Chakra Healing. 1999 Sterling Publishing Company, New York.

Sree Chakravarti. A Healer's Journey. 1993, Rudra Press, Portland, OR.

Swami Rama. Rudolf Balantine, Alan Hymes, MD. The Science of Breath. 1979 The Himalayan International Institute, Honesdale, Pennsylvania.

Swami Sada Shiva Tirtha. The Ayurveda Encyclopedia. 1998, Sri Satguru Publications.

Swami Sivananda Radha. Mantras, Words of Power. 1980, Sterling Publishers, PVT. LTD.

Swami Sivananda. The Science of Pranayama. Divine Life Society, Himalayas India.

Swami Venkatesananda. The Concise Yoga Vasistha. State University of New York Press, Albany New York 1984.

Tansley, D. Chakras – Rays and Radionics. The C.W. Daniel Company Limited, Essex, England. 1984.

Tansley, David. Radionics and the Subtle Anatomy of Man. 1971, Great Britain, Whitstable Litho LTD, Whitstable, Kent, England.

Tansley, David. Subtle Bodies, Essence and Shadow. 1985, Thames and Hudson, Great Britain.

Tansley, David. The Raiment of Light, A study of the human aura. 1984.

Thich Nhat Hanh. The Heart of the Buddhas Teaching. 1988, Parallax Press, Berkeley, California.

Willis, Pauline. Color Therapy. 1993 Element Books Limited, Shaftesbury, Dorset, England, SP78BP.

Wood, E. The Seven Rays. 1985. Reprint. Theosophical Publishing House, Wheaton, IL 1984.

Worwood, Valerie Ann. The Fragrant Mind – Aromatherapy for Personality, Mind, Mood and Emotions. New World Library, Novato, California 1996.

Zinn, Jon Kabat. Wherever you go there you are, mindfulness meditations in everyday life. 1994, Hyperion 114 Fifth Avenue, New York, New York 10001.

Vibrational Remedies Suppliers

Nelson Bach USA, Ltd.
100 Research Drive
Wilmington, MA 01887
1-800-319-9151
http://www.nelsonbach.com/usa.html

Flower Essence Services
PO Box 1769
Nevada City, CA 95959
1-800-548-0075
www.floweressence.com

Alaskan Flower Essence Project
PO Box 1329
Homer, AL 99603
907-235-2188

Australian Bush Flower Essences
Box 531
Spit Junction, NSW
2088 Australia
www.ausflowers.com.au

Ellon, USA, Inc
644 Merrick Road
Lynbrook, NY, 11563
516-593-2206

Perelandra, Ltd.
P.O. Box 3603
Warrenton, VA 20188
1-800-960-8806
www.perelandra-ltd.com

Vibrational Remedies Suppliers – continued

Pegasus Products, Inc
PO Box 228
Boulder, CO 80306
1-800-527-6104
www.pegasusproducts.com

Living Essences of Australia
P.O. Box 355
Scarborough W.A. 6019
Australia
Tel#:+61 8 94435600
http://www.livingessences.com.au

Desert Alchemy Essences
PO Box 44189
Tucson, AZ 85733
1-800-736-3382
www.desert-alchemy.com

3 Flowers Healing
Aromatherapy, Columbia River Gorge
Flower Essences and Gaia Lotion
541-387-3528
www.3flowershealing.com

Tara Mandala's Herbs
www.taramandala.com

Wise Woman Herbals
541-895-5152
www.medherb.com

Sound Healing Resources
www.healingsounds.com

Edmund Scientific Company
101 Gloucester Pike
Barrington, NJ 08007
609-573-6250

Dinshah Health Society
100 Dinshah Drive
Malaga, NJ, 08328
609-692-4686

Tools for Exploration
Independence Avenue
Chatsworth, CA 91311-4318
818-885-9090
www.toolsforexploration.com
Source for light and sound therapy
instruments.
www.doorwaypublications.com
good pendulum source

The L.I.F.E. System
Jennifer Walton 520-297-0336
A unique and highly effective
biofeedback program that can
provide direction and focus in
vibrational assessment and treatment.

Sanjeevani Remedies & Remedy
Cards
G-Jo Institute
PO Box 848060
Hollywood, Fl. 33084-9755
Based on the teachings of Sathya Sai
Baba, this prayer system of healing is
free. Using prayer along with radionic
symbols, healing codes are sent
through the scalor wave to the
recipient.

Energy Medicine Resources, Research, Information & Websites

Alternative Medicine Home Page
http://www.pitt.edu/~cbw/
mailing.html

Better Health Campaign
www.betterhealthcampaign.org

Center for Health and Healing
www.healthandhealingny.org

Consumer Health Organization of
Canada
www.consumerhealth.org

Larry Dossey, MD
Author and educator in alternative
health therapies.
www.dosseydossey.com

Dr. David Hawkins M.D., Ph.D.
The Institute for Advanced Spiritual
Research
P.O. Box 3516 W. Sedona, AZ 86340
928-282-8722
www.sedonacreativelife.com
www.veritaspub.com
Research on kinesiological testing as a
tool for assessing value, motive, truth
and path of consciousness as a race and
as individuals.

Kinesiologists United
P.O. Box 48957
Coon Rapids, MN 55448-0957
1-877-581-1678
www.kinesiologycentral.com

Bruce Lipton Ph.D.
Uncovering the Biology of Belief.
www.brucelipton.com
Biomedical sciences research
proving how holistic therapies work.

Dr. Caroline Myss
www.myss.com
Online resource directory &
education source

National Center for Complimentary
and Alternative Medicine
http://nccam.nih.gov

Wholistic Healing Research
www.wholistichealingresearch.com
Cutting edge research on energy,
medicine, consciousness.

Spiritual & Energy Healing Centers, Schools & Resources

Dynapro International, Inc.
PO Box 3002, Ogden, UT 84409
Order- 1-800-877-1413

Omega Institute for Holistic Studies
www.eomega.org

Esalen Institute
Highway 1
Big Sur, CA 93920-9616
831-667-3000
http://www.esalen.org

Institute of Noetic Sciences
101 San Antonio Road
Petaluma, CA 94952 USA
707.775.3500
www.noetic.org

Institute of Transpersonal
Psychology
1069 East Meadow Circle
Palo Alto CA, 94303
650-493-4430
www.itp.edu

Natural Therapies/Schools Directory
www.naturalhealers.com

International Society for the Study of
Subtle Energies and Energy Medicine
11005 Ralston Road, Suite 100D •
Arvada, CO 80004
Voice: 303-425-4625
www.issseem.org

Intuition Network
http://www.intuition.org

Barbara Brennan School of Natural
Healing
PO Box 2005
East Hampton, NY 11937
1-800-924-2564

Colorado Center for Healing Touch
& Healing Touch International
www.healingtouch.net

The Chopra Center
www.chopra.com
Depak Chopra's Wellness Center

Hollyhock
www.hollyhock.bc.ca
Conference and Retreat Center

IM School of Healing Arts
www.imschool.com

Brietenbush Hot Springs
www.brietenbush.com
Conference and Retreat Center

Mt. Madonna Spiritual Center
http://www.mountmadonna.org
Conference and Retreat Center

Kairos Institute of Sound Healing
157 Pacheco Rd., Box 8
Llano de San Juan, NM 87543
Phone: 505-587-2689
www.acutonics.com

Touch For Health®Kinesiology
Association
PO Box 392
New Carlisle, Oh 45344-0392
800-466-8342
www.tfhka.org

Quantum Touch
P.O. Box 458
Kapaa, HI 96746
888-424-0041
www.quantumtouch.com

Dr. Eric Pearl
Reconnective Healing
www.thereconnection.com

Findhorn Foundation
www.findhorn.org
Wholistic Educational Center and
community

Theosophical Society of America
www.theosophical.org
Classes, workshops and retreats.

Amachi
www.amma.org
Spiritual Teacher

Sri Satya Sai Baba
www.sathyasai.org
Spiritual Teacher

Lorian Association
P.O. Box 1368
Issaquah, WA. 98027
435-427-9071
http://www.lorian.org
Spiritual Education in the
Findhorn community tradition

Emotional Freedom Technique
www.emofree.com
Classes, videos, and practitioners
of Tapping Treatment

The Energy Medicine Institute
www.energymed.org

Holfield Institute
5275 S. April Dr.
Langley, WA 98260
360-321-7226
http://www.holfieldinstitute.org
Training in Field Dynamics for
practitioners in service profes-
sions

Circles of Life – Solutions
www.circlesoflife.com
Products to enhance well-being
and quality of life. "The strength
of one can empower the many."

Jaya Sarada, PhD, offers Well Being Sessions, Energy Readings, *Life Essence Awakening Process* ™, Certified EFT sessions (emotional freedom technique) Practioner, Spiritual Counseling and Intuitive Readings either in person or telephone consultation. She is available for seminars, retreats, book signings, lectures and guest speaking engagements. Please call for to inquire or make an appointment. Well Being Foundation: 1-800-282-5292.

Jaya Sarada is a teacher of Holistic Healing and Life Transformation methods such as; Kinesiology, Acupressure, Aura Healing, Vibrational Medicine, Energy Field Kinesiology and Intuitive Counseling. She is the founder of the *Well Being Foundation*, a non-profit organization devoted to developing programs for the healing and transformation of the body, mind and spirit. Jaya is also the founder of *Well Being Institute*, a school for training and certification in energy healing and counseling for the health of the body, mind and spirit.

Jaya Sarada has dedicated her life to the search for truth and holds a PhD in Transpersonal Psychology, as well as being a practicing minister in healing and counseling. Jaya offers counseling, energy balancing and intuitive readings and EFT (Emotional Freedom Technique) by appointment, either in person or by telephone. The innovative techniques she has created serve to identify areas of constricted energy and corresponding methods of release.

Jaya is the author of three other books about energy healing, *Trust in Yourself—Messages from the Divine, The Path of Return—The Light of Parashakti*, and *Living Meditations*.

For information on training, certification programs, speaking schedule or appointments, please contact Jaya Sarada:

Well Being Foundation
PO Box 1081
Freeland, WA 98249
(800) 282-5292
www.wellbeinginstitute.org
www.wellbeingfoundation.org

Index

From the unreal, lead me to the real
From the darkness, lead me to the light
From death, lead me to immortality

Om Shanti, Om Shanti, Om Shanti

Qty	Item	Cost	S&H	Total
	Books by Jaya Sarada:			
	Trust in Yourself - Messages from the Divine	13.95	5.00	18.95
	The Path of Return - The Light of Parashakti	16.95	5.00	21.95
	Life Essence Awakening (Books available for wholesale in quantity more than 10, please call for information)	37.00	8.00	45.00
	Color Glasses - 7 (*red, green, blue, yellow, orange, indigo, violet*)	75.00		
	Color Glasses - 9 (*red, green, blue, yellow, orange, indigo, violet, magenta, turquoise*)	95.00		
	Set of 15 Colored Charts (*Seven chakras, energy anatomy and planes of consciousness*)	30.00	5.00	35.00
	Well Being in Body, Mind and Spirit	39.95		
	LEAP 1 Video - The Etheric Field	39.95		
	LEAP 2 Video - The Emotional and Mental Fields	39.95		
	LEAP 3 Video - Soul Kinesiology *Coming soon: LEAP Vibrational Toolbox Remedies Guided meditations and books on tape also coming soon!*	39.95		

Further information available at:

www.wellbeinginstitute.org

Sub Total _____

Shipping Total _____

Tax _____

Order Total _____

Method of Payment:
AE VISA MC Discover   Check_____

CC#_____ Expiration_____

Name:_____

Shipping Address:_____

City, State, Zip_____

Phone: (_____)_____-_____

Please contact Customer Service at 1-800-282-5292 to confirm order.
Online ordering is currently not available. Wholesale inquiries welcome.

Printed in the United States
37410LVS00006B/51-54

9 781893 037021